CURRICULUM TECHNOLOGY
Patrol Procedures in the USA

CONTRIBUTORS:

Melissa Cahill, Daryl Davis, Steve DeBoard,
Julie Gibson, Karl Johnson, Mike Marcon and Dave West

EDITOR:

Jennifer-Lynn Jennings

CHANNEL CUSTOM PUBLISHING

Photography: All photographs courtesy of Curriculum Technology and iStockphoto.com.

Publisher: Channel Custom, 3520 Seagate Way, Suite 115, Oceanside, CA 92056.

Manufactured in the United States of America, 1st edition, Curriculum Technology, LLC, 2011.

Patrol Procedures in the USA. A textbook by Curriculum Technology, LLC. Oceanside, CA. 1st edition, 2011.

ISBN 978-0-9830949-9-9

WARNING: Re-creation of any case study or event listed in the materials may result in injury or property damage if extensive care is not taken at all times. Curriculum Technology and Channel Publishing are not responsible for any injuries or damage to property that may occur from the use of referenced equipment or any other supplies.

Experiments and activities derived from this book should be conducted with oversight by, and at the direction of, a qualified instructor.
***

Other Titles in Curriculum Technology's USA Textbook Series

CJ Communications in the USA

CJ in the USA: An Introduction to Criminal Justice

CJ Investigations in the USA

Homeland Security in the USA: A Student Handbook

Also available: e-courses designed in conjunction with these textbooks

Curriculum Technology Interactive Modules (iMods)

iMods are focused instructional units that provide instructors and students with the application of knowledge and job skills used every day by professionals in the workplace. Meant to supplement academic theory learned in the classroom, iMods provide the connection of that theory to practical application, helping to create a rich and engaging learning environment.

Current Titles in the Criminal Justice iMod Series:

Fingerprint Science and Live Scan

Video Surveillance

Security Planning and Prevention

Drugs and their Effects

Jobs in Justice and Security

Tactical Communications

Criminology

Courtroom Layout and Procedure

Handcuff Basics

Applying Handcuffs

Waist Chains and Leg Shackles

Plastic Restraints and Maintenance

Transportation and Jail Facility Layout

For further information, please visit:

http://www.curriculumtechnology.com

About the Contributors

Melissa Cahill, MA.Ed

Melissa Cahill has professional law enforcement and educational career spanning over 22 years, including nine years in probation, 10 years in policing and 8 years as an educator. She received her Bachelor's degree in Criminal Justice with a minor in Sociology, and her Masters of Arts in Education. Her specialties include curriculum development, weaponless defense, firearms and law enforcement communications.

During her probation career she worked with and developed rehabilitation programs for incarcerated juveniles, court investigations and supervision of adult high-risk gang offenders. While working as a Reserve Police Sergeant, she worked Patrol, Vice, Narcotics, Background Investigations and specialized in Gang Suppression.

She is currently a Division Manager at a private college, where she writes statewide curriculum pertaining to Criminal Justice, First Responders and other programs. She is also a Criminal Justice professor at Taft Community College. She continues to write Criminal Justice curriculum for educational institutions across the United States.

Daryl Davis

Daryl Davis is a Sergeant in the Protective Services Department of the Santa Clara Valley Health and Hospital System in Santa Clara County, California. Originally from Chicago, Daryl attended Stanford University and earned his Bachelor's degree in Political Science. He graduated from Police Academy at San Jose City College. His career includes stints in Patrol, Corrections, Court Security, Investigations,

Personnel & Training, Crowd Control, and Search & Rescue. Daryl is a POST-certified Field Training Officer and holds instructor certifications in firearms, baton, arrest control techniques, and OC Spray. He is certified as a Terrorism Liaison Officer, an instructor in Incident Response to Terrorist Bombing and Prevention and Response to Suicide Bombing Incidents, and the Crisis Intervention Team (CIT). He has a background in computer systems, network support and cyber security. He is married and the father of twin daughters.

Steve DeBoard, MS

Steve DeBoard's experience includes 35 years in the criminal justice industry, 21 of which were working with the Indianapolis Police Department. Steve served in the patrol division and worked the majority of years on the department in investigations. As an investigator, Steve worked in Vice, Sex Crimes and Homicide. Prior to his current position in higher education as a department chair at Kaplan College, Steve taught Criminal Justice courses at ITT Technical Institute. As the Director of Public Safety at Olivet Nazarene University in Bourbonnais, IL, he instituted the Incident Management protocol for the campus community. He is currently implementing an incident management procedure for Kaplan College in Indianapolis, IN.

Mr. DeBoard holds a Bachelor of Science in Management and a Masters of Science in Justice and Security Administration. Steve has been working on a PhD in Public Safety Leadership, serves on Curriculum Technology's Criminal Justice National Advisory Board.

Julie Gibson, MD, MBA, RN

Julie received her MD from Southern Illinois University School of Medicine. She was a registered nurse with seven years experience in a neonatal intensive care unit prior to completing medical school, where she specialized in forensic pathology and pediatrics. Dr. Gibson has been a medical examiner in Maricopa County,

Arizona (Phoenix) and the Chief Medical Examiner of Mohave County, Arizona. She has Master's degrees in Human Behavior and Business, and Bachelor's degrees in Psychology and Biology.

Dr. Gibson has responded to multiple mass fatality disasters as a member of the federal Disaster Mortuary Operational Response Team (DMORT) and is a member of DMORT-WMD, a specialty HAZMAT team responsible for recovering and decontaminating bodies following weapons of mass destruction incidents under U.S. Health and Human Services.

Dr. Gibson teaches Impact of Disaster for Western Washington University, teaches Forensic Nursing for Kaplan University, teaches medicine to medical students at A.T. Still University in Mesa, Arizona, and is a pediatric urgent care physician at Good Night Pediatrics in Phoenix, Arizona. She formerly taught Criminal Justice classes. She is Arizona POST certified in handguns and shotguns, has gone through the citizen's police academy, and volunteers as an armed posse member for the Maricopa County Sheriff's Office. She is a member of the National Criminal Justice Board, and is a member of the Commission for Forensic Education.

Karl Johnson

Karl Johnson spent 12 years in Corrections and Law Enforcement in urban California. His police experience includes Patrol, Jail Operations and Prisoner Transportation, as well as SWAT Operations and Training. After the September 11, 2011 attacks, he became a contractor to the US State Department and other government agencies, providing personal security services to diplomats and others. He also trained local security and police agencies in several countries in the Middle East and Central Asia. He lives in North Carolina.

Mike Marcon

Mike Marcon is a retired Tactical Medic, Special Weapons and Tactics (SWAT) operator, Advanced Life Support Provider and Emergency Management specialist. His diverse career includes Chemical, Biological, Radiological and Nuclear Emergency Services, Military Police Operations, and Protective Security Specialist Operations. He has also served in Undercover and Urban Patrol capacities.

Dave West, BS, CPP

Dave West is the Director of International Security Operations with a Virginia-based firm that specializes in providing law enforcement, security advisory and training services to the US Department of State and US Department of Defense. Originally from Memphis, Tennessee, he attended Memphis State University and received his Bachelors of Science in Education. He also holds a Masters Certificate in Project Management from the University of Tennessee, and a Masters Certificate in Business Administration from Heriot Watt University. He is a Board Certified Protection Professional (CPP) through the American Society for Industrial Security (ASIS) and has been a member of the ASIS Council on Business Practices since 2009. A former law enforcement officer, he has worked assignments within his agency's Fugitive Apprehension Squad, Special Weapons and Tactics Team (SWAT), and within Uniform Patrol. He holds over twenty law enforcement instructor and master instructor certifications from a variety of state, federal, and private organizations including, but not limited to the FBI, Tennessee POST, Arkansas POST, and the NRA.

Table of Contents

MODULE 1

Police Agency Structures

Key Module Concepts:

- How public accountability affects police agencies

- The source of police authority

- A typical agency's chain of command

- The need for special units

- Tasks that various special units perform

Introduction

All American police agencies derive their authority from the law. This applies to agencies of every size, from small rural departments to urban agencies with many officers. The laws Americans must follow, and which all police departments must enforce, originate in the United States Constitution and work their way down into state laws and local city ordinances. Unlike many countries where the police and military are comprised of one organization, American law enforcement officers are civilians who are responsible to both the laws they uphold and the people they serve.

Law enforcement agencies are **paramilitary** organizations, which means that they follow, to some extent, military organizational models with ranks and clear chains of command. As modern law enforcement becomes more complex, and as technology becomes more a part of both criminal activity and crime fighting, specialized units using officers and other employees with special skills and training are becoming more necessary.

In this Module, you'll learn how law enforcement agencies are organized and authorized in the United States. The examples given are not universally applicable, because each state is responsible for making its own rules, which are based on local needs while remaining within the limits defined by federal law. However, the examples given are valid in most of the country. Within this Module, the term "police department" applies to other law enforcement agencies, such as sheriff's departments, while "corrections" refers to the operation of local, state, or federal jails and prisons.

Ask Yourself

- *Who decides what city or town gets a police department?*
- *What does "chain of command" mean with regard to law enforcement?*
- *What is the purpose of special units within police departments?*

Who Gets A Police Department?

You may be surprised to find that there are a number of police agencies in your state, as well as a variety of jurisdictions that have law enforcement agencies. Certainly, you are used to police departments working for cities, sheriff's departments in most of the counties, and state police agencies with highway patrolmen or "troopers," but there are many other opportunities in this career field.

Each state is left to determine how its law enforcement officers are defined, trained, recruited and used, as long as the state does not contradict federal, or national, law. This local authority stems from two historical features present at the nation's development:

- The Founding Fathers' philosophical preference for leaving any governmental duties not touching on international affairs and interstate commerce to the jurisdiction of the states

- The difficulty of rapid travel for personnel and communication of information over long distances in a nation as large as the U.S.

Because of this concept of a **decentralized government**, which allows services and decisions to be made at the lowest possible level of government, each state is allowed great latitude in determining exactly what sort of police agencies it needs to serve its citizens without local police functions being managed by federal authorities.

This local control allows for the best use of resources for local needs. Even within a single state, there are both large cities and rural areas, each with different budgets for police services. **Incorporation** is the term used when a state recognizes a city or town and gives it the right to form its own government, also known as a **municipal government**. These municipal governments have the authority to create law enforcement departments to provide public services, but there are other organizations that can do the same thing.

For instance, in most states, both public and private schools and universities can operate police departments to serve their institutions' needs. Most large public transit organizations have a law enforcement unit, as do many park systems and even unincorporated gated communities. Generally, an organization that is allowed to provide police services can operate its own department, contract for police services with a neighboring city's police department or the county sheriff's office, or contract with a company that provides private police services. The requirements for the hiring and training of private police vary widely by state, as does the authority granted to private police officers.

Accountability To The Public

The vast majority of police officers in the U.S. work for departments operated by the municipal governments of incorporated towns, cities, and counties. These local agencies fill the needs for police services specific to their area of responsibility, or **jurisdiction**. In some states, police officers have the same authority throughout the state that they do in their home cities, while in other jurisdictions, the authority is divided between different departments. Even if state laws stretch their authority across the state, police officers can expect to do the vast majority of their work in their home jurisdiction.

All police officers and departments are accountable to their employers in various ways. Obviously, an individual officer who fails to fulfill his responsibilities can be fired, but what about an entire department? Although it most commonly happens due to budgetary shortfalls, entire police departments can be, and are, dissolved when the community they serve no longer trusts them.

City and Town Police Departments

The size of a city or town's police departments is dictated by the needs of the city's population. New York City, for example, has over 34,000 officers in its police department, but most law enforcement departments throughout the country have fewer than 20 officers on staff.

Accountability, or answering to the public for actions taken by the department, begins with the police chief. The city's governing body, such as a mayor, usually appoints a police chief; they are rarely elected officials. If a police department is ineffective, corrupt, or loses the trust of the city's residents for any reason, the chief is usually the first to feel the pressure. As appointed officials, police chiefs can be fired by the city council, or they can be penalized through the use of the budgetary process. The behavior of department personnel is the chief's responsibility.

Many large urban departments have some form of **oversight committee** made up of members of the community they serve. The authority given to these committees varies, but most are limited to making advisory suggestions, rather than being able to change policies themselves. Committees such as these exist to provide a voice for public concerns about how police work is accomplished; they also provide a venue for the department to explain its operations to the public.

Individual officers are, of course, responsible for the work they perform, or fail to perform. Just as police officers are not always correct, complaints made by accused criminals must also be taken with some skepticism. A department's **internal affairs unit** is the first to investigate allegations of misconduct, and it must be aware that its investigation may be closely examined in court or in the media. Officers can protect themselves from false accusations with careful and complete documentation of incidents, and through the increasing use of cameras and voice recordings of incidents.

County Sheriff's Department

The **sheriff** is an elected official of the county in which he serves. In most states, the **sheriff's department**, which is responsible for law enforcement in unincorporated areas of the county, and the deputy sheriffs who are employed by it share the same legal authority as a city police officer. However, some states limit their authority and responsibilities. An elected official is always dependent on maintaining the trust of the voters in order to stay in office. A trusted sheriff can be re-elected many times, but one who is not trustworthy can be removed by the voters in the next election, or even, in extreme cases, in special elections.

The sheriff is usually responsible for the operation of a county's jails, as well as providing security for the courts and for the transportation of inmates between jail and court. Many sheriffs also have patrol functions in cities that contract with the sheriff for their services.

These services are complex, and the sheriff must walk a tightrope, ensuring that incarcerated individuals are afforded the rights and services the law requires, without offending the voters who have to pay for what they might consider unnecessary services and facilities. Cities contracting with the sheriff for police services can always find another provider or start their own police department if the sheriff's services are inadequate or too expensive.

Individual deputies are accountable to the public in the same way as city police officers; those who work in jails are also held responsible for guaranteeing the rights, health and safety of those in their care.

Other Departments and Private Police

There is a third class of police department that is more limited than the city or county level police departments. This class includes police departments employed by schools and colleges, transit districts or housing authorities, and **private police** employed by communities or businesses.

Each state has different laws that define the role of these agencies. In some states, every law enforcement officer, no matter what his or her specific job, must have the same basic training, while in others the training is more closely related to specific job requirements. Regardless of the training required, each of these agencies employs law enforcement officers with police powers in force, at least while the officer is on duty in the agency's jurisdiction.

For example, police officers assigned to departments at schools, housing authorities, or hospitals are working an area much like a small town's police department. The officers are usually known, at least by sight, to the employees, residents, and long-term students. While they are expected to keep the peace on campus, they are not generally expected to intervene except when an individual's safety is at risk. If even one officer gains a reputation for being heavy-handed or even disagreeable, the department's ability to perform its mission suffers.

Private police departments are controversial in many places, with detractors claiming that these departments do not have adequate public accountability because they are not public employees. This is likely only partly true, as the companies that provide private police services must continually fulfill contracted requirements and periodically bid to keep their contracts. They will simply be replaced if the department is not responsive to its employers. There is always a concern that the employer might require their private police department to engage in unlawful conduct; the history of using company police as strike breakers, for example, is well known. With today's stronger civil rights laws, and the likelihood that misconduct will be recorded and posted on the Internet, both contracting companies and private police providers have much to lose in the court of public opinion.

Chain Of Command

One of the reasons that police departments are often described as paramilitary organizations is their use of a military-like chain of command. A **chain of command** is the line that orders follow, extending from the police chief or sheriff through to the officer required to carry out that order. Generally, orders are given down the chain one level at a time, and if an officer runs into trouble following a specific order, then his resource for help is an officer on the immediate level above him.

Though rank structures may vary between departments, in general they use a system similar to the military's. The department's executive, whether chief or sheriff, is at the top, with assistant chiefs or assistant sheriffs, who report directly to the executive, directly below. Below the assistant chief or sheriff are captains, lieutenants, sergeants, and then officers/deputies. Larger departments may add more ranks, and smaller ones use less, but the idea of a chain of command is maintained.

The chain of command is more than just a way to pass orders. By assigning a sergeant to supervise a certain number of patrol officers within a specific geographical area, a team is created that can be controlled as situations require. The number of officers assigned per sergeant is dependent on the type of work they are doing, and it may change from one division to another. For example, a sergeant might be able to properly supervise six patrol deputies, but he has twelve deputies working in a single high-rise jail building. This concept is called **span of control**; it originated in military management studies and has been adopted by civilian police departments. Even corporate operations have made use of this concept.

In a major emergency, many agencies might have to band together to manage the crisis. The **Incident Command System (ICS)** is a standardized plan allowing departments that have never worked together to come together effectively. The chain of command ICS implements has assigned responsibilities and lines of communication in a clear and unambiguous way.

Resource - The Incident Command System is a nationwide standardized incident response plan intended to allow individuals from police, fire, EMS, and other rescue agencies to work together in a major emergency.

The response to Hurricane Katrina is an example of a situation in which ICS is invaluable. Police officers from California to New York responded to assist in Louisiana, and fire departments from around the country also arrived, often without the incident commander being aware they were coming. They were incorporated into the response plan and assigned duties and a place in the chain of command quickly and efficiently.

http://www.fema.gov/emergency/nims/IncidentCommand System.shtm

CASE STUDY

A department's chain of command is apparent in its organizational chart. Each agency develops its own organizational plan based on the number of employees it has and their responsibilities.

Review the chart used by the small police department serving Nichols Hills, Oklahoma. **http://www.nicholshills.net/Page.asp?NavID=75**

This small agency has just a few ranks, and a very easily followed chain of command. It is important to realize that each box in the chart refers to a position within the organization, and not necessarily to an individual employee. One sergeant, for example, may perform the responsibilities of two of the sergeant boxes if another is on vacation (or if a new sergeant is being selected or trained), or the assistant chief may perform the duties assigned to the empty sergeant's box in the chain. Either way, the line of communication and chain of command are clear to everyone involved.

Compare this to the much more complex organizational chart of the very large Los Angeles Police Department. **http://www.lapdonline.org/ inside_the_lapd/content_basic_view/1063**

In an agency this size, to create a chart in which every employee has a visible space would require many pages and be too complex to be useful, so this chart only goes down to the level of captain. Each division that is led by a captain named on the chart will have its own chart, so the line of communication and chain of command can be followed from the executive all the way down. In a department of this size, officers seldom hear directly from or even see the chief, but they are aware of the portion of the chart they are most directly attached to.

FIGURE 1.1: *There are many specializations under the umbrella of law enforcement.*

Police Special Units

There was a day when a police officer walked a portion of a town alone. People had to walk everywhere unless they were wealthy enough to afford horses, so they tended to be limited in the areas of the city they would visit. The "cop on the beat" knew almost everyone in his area by sight, and quickly learned who was likely to break laws, and in what way, and he was alerted to any unknown visitors who did not seem to have legitimate business in his precinct.

When automobiles became more affordable for the general population, the shape of cities changed, and so did the means needed to police them. Among the first of the **police special units** were automobiles using "flying squads," which waited at a central point until they were dispatched to assist beat cops all over town. Over time, telephone and radio technology advancements allowed beat cops to communicate to a dispatch center and mobile units almost immediately. In the U.S., police departments have always tried to use advancing technology to do their jobs more effectively and safely for themselves, suspects, and the citizens at large.

Modern special units follow that tradition, and are now such a fixture in movies and TV shows that most people can't believe that SWAT teams and CSI units are very recent developments in police agencies. This dicussion will cover three categories of special units:

- Operations
- Technology/Science
- Investigations

These divisions are simply for convenience; one is not more or less important than another. The work of all the sworn officers and non-sworn technicians is equally important to keep the public safe and to catch and prosecute criminals.

Operations

The operations division is the public face of the police. These are the uniformed officers using marked vehicles, and they are the first to respond to an emergency call. Within the operations category are those who do patrol, SWAT, K9, jail services, and community outreach efforts.

Patrol

Patrol officers, including traffic enforcement specialists, are those people with whom the public has the most contact. They respond to calls for service in emergency and routine matters, take the first reports from victims and witnesses, and initiate contacts when they see dangerous or illegal activity during their patrols. Many citizens would be surprised to find how many wanted suspects and dangerous criminals are identified and captured during a routine traffic stop. Patrol is where nearly all police officers start their careers, and where most city officers spend their careers. Before they are allowed to participate in more specialized units, officers must prove they have mastered the basics of patrol work.

Traffic specialists are patrol officers who have received extra training in the enforcement of vehicle laws, as well as in accident reconstruction. Although they are detailed specifically to enforce traffic laws, their task is not, as many would suggest, simply to collect revenue. By stopping drivers who are engaged in dangerous behavior on the road, traffic officers save lives that might otherwise be lost to irresponsible drivers who have forgotten that their vehicles are potentially dangerous weapons.

SWAT

SWAT was created in the late 1960s by the Los Angeles Police Department in response to several sniping incidents around the country and an escalation of violence against police. SWAT, which stands for Special Weapons And Tactics, may be called ERT (Emergency Response Team), CIRT (Critical Incident Response Team), or any number of other names. No matter what the name, the concept is the same.

SWAT is called in for situations that patrol officers are not equipped or trained to handle. They handle incidents such as hostage crises, high-risk arrests or search warrants, and VIP protection. They are trained in the use of weapons and tools over and above those given to regular patrol officers. Some teams even have armored vehicles used to transport team members safely through areas where they could potentially be shot.

Officers who are chosen for SWAT training must first prove to be competent, motivated, and disciplined in their previous assignments. Most SWAT teams are not full-time teams, but rather draw their members from throughout the department, often from officers who train and practice together, but who work normal patrol or other tasks between calls.

FIGURE 1.2: *K-9 units are increasingly important to a number of police activities.*

K9

Police dogs have been used by law enforcement for many years. Canine (K9) units are invaluable when searching for hidden suspects, and for finding drugs, explosives, and almost any other substances with odors they are trained to recognize.

Police dogs are highly trained and very expensive assets to the department. The usual image of a police dog is a German Shepherd or similar breed trained to chase down suspects and either bite and hold, or bark and hold the suspect until the human partner can catch up to the scene. The officers who work with these dogs are required to go through extensive training where they learn to maintain the dog's health and to reinforce its training throughout its working life.

Seen less often are dogs trained to use their very sensitive noses to find things that are not easily found. Many dogs are trained to sniff out drugs or explosives; while sometimes a patrol dog can be cross trained to be an effective search dog, various breeds with noses more sensitive than a Shepherd's are more frequently used. One advantage to using a smaller breed is that they can access areas a larger dog cannot, and can even be lifted by their handlers into high areas or over fences. Dogs can also be trained for search and rescue, finding people trapped in the rubble of collapsed buildings and locating the bodies of murder victims.

In many states, harming a police dog while it is working carries much higher penalties than simple animal cruelty charges. Some agencies consider their dogs to be sworn members of the department, and they issue badges and ID cards to members of K9 units. Police dogs are often given formal police funerals if killed in the line of duty.

FIGURE 1.3: *Employees of sheriff's departments are frequently responsible for prisoner transport.*

Jails

In much of the U.S., local jails are under the control of the county sheriff, and most deputy sheriffs start their careers here. Running a jail, populated by a potentially uncooperative set of inmates, is a complex task. Deputies and corrections officers must learn the indicators that will allow them to prevent fights and disruptions, or to react quickly if they are already underway. Men and women in jail awaiting trial or serving their sentences are under considerable stress, and are apt to act out in various ways that could be self-destructive or harmful to someone else.

Anything that can happen in the real world can happen inside a jail. Weapons may be smuggled in, or made out of materials available to the inmates. Drugs are smuggled into the prison in various ways and trafficked within the walls. Large county agencies may even have specialized SWAT teams and K9 units trained to operate in the confines of a jail facility.

The sheriff is usually responsible for transporting inmates to and from court dates and to medical appointments outside the facility. Transportation of inmates is a specialized and challenging duty in itself.

Community Outreach

Law enforcement departments and the people they serve have to work closely together for good results. Community outreach programs are intended to keep lines of communication open, and to provide contact with police officers not related to arrests.

An increasingly common outreach program is the Citizen's Police Academy, where members of the public can get a feel for the complexity of modern police work. These classes and ride-alongs with patrol officers help bridge the gap between the two groups, and encourage an educated dialogue between the police and those they serve.

Other outreach programs are designed to address specific problems identified by community members, or to demonstrate extra efforts to serve ethnic populations that tend to be suspicious of police. Police officers may receive extra training so that they can work with nurses and social workers to provide services to members of the community who suffer from mental illnesses. These efforts are made to keep the mentally ill out of the criminal justice system and in the mental health system, where they can receive appropriate help.

Outreach to juveniles is designed to reduce the use of drugs and alcohol among minors, and to humanize the police and criminal justice system to young people who probably have little to no positive exposure in this area. In many states, juveniles caught committing minor crimes, such as missing curfew or petty theft, can be diverted from the criminal justice system into an informal probation program monitored by the police department.

Science And Technology

Police departments depend on a large number of technicians and other employees with specialized training and experience to track the vast amounts of information and evidence necessary for investigations and prosecutions. Although they are not generally sworn officers themselves, technicians who operate the fingerprint and photo identification offices, crime labs, and records units work behind the scenes to provide officers with the information they need in order to be both safe and effective in their jobs.

Identification

Fingerprints are still the most common type of positive identification used in the criminal justice system. While the use of electronic fingerprint records has sped up the process dramatically, the skills and experience of the technicians are still the most important and effective part of the process.

Fingerprints are impressions left by ridges on human fingers, and they have been recognized as unique identifiers for thousands of years. However, they have only been used in the U.S. for criminal identification purposes for about a century. Different systems have been used to differentiate one print from another, comparing the features and distinctive patterns formed by the ridges on a suspect's fingers. It is imperative that technicians have extensive training in recognizing these patterns. Even with the complex classification system used in the U.S., called the *Henry System of Classification*, it could take years for a technician to become truly efficient in pattern recognition. Fortunately, computers have taken over the day-to-day work of fingerprint identification, but skilled and experienced humans are still required to handle prints that are not computer readable. Fingerprint impressions are taken from every person booked after arrest; this creates a large collection of known prints and identities. Each time a person is arrested, his or her fingerprints are compared with those taken during their last arrest to ensure that they are still who they claim to be. Before computerized fingerprint comparison was common, getting a manual verification could take hours if the technicians were busy. Now the confirmation comes back in seconds because the computer only has to compare two sets of prints.

Prints found at crime scenes, even if complete and clear, must be compared with all prints in the records, so those identifications can take considerably longer. Even so, the wait is measured in hours, which differs from the past, when identification was done manually and took days or weeks to complete. Computerized fingerprints can now be rolled in the field and transmitted electronically for positive suspect identification without ever having to bring the suspect into the jail or police department. Fingerprints that rule out suspects are just as valuable as those that confirm the guilt of suspects.

Modern computer technology has also made face recognition and classification possible, which opens a whole new set of opportunities for identification bureaus. Other permanent identifying features, such as tattoos, birthmarks, or missing limbs, can also be photographed or described for future comparison.

Records

Another behind-the-scenes aspect of the criminal justice system is the records division, which is comprised of the skilled clerks and technicians who operate it. There is no way a patrol officer can be aware of all the arrest warrants active in a city, especially those active in other jurisdictions.

When a patrol officer stops a speeding driver or makes any arrest, the records division checks that suspect's history to see if he or she is a wanted criminal or has a history of violence against the police. This is certainly important information for the involved officer to know. Other information, such as driver's license status and car registration information, is also readily available.

The records division's work does not end at an arrest. They also keep track of a suspect's status in the court process, when they are next expected to be in court, and, if already sentenced, what their release date is. Corrections officers need this information so they know who must be transferred to court hearings, and ensure that convicted inmates are incarcerated for their entire sentence, but not a moment longer.

Crime Lab

Some large departments have their own crime labs, but usually they are regional or state run entities employing non-sworn scientists and technicians. Along with their scientific knowledge, these employees must understand the legal rules of evidence, and be dedicated to following them carefully if the evidence they process is to be of any value in court.

Unlike TV dramas, the lab workers are seldom the same people as those who collect the evidence from a scene. Typically, evidence is collected by police officers. However, many large departments employ non-sworn evidence collection technicians, who work with officers and detectives to collect evidence properly, some of which might be sent to a lab for further study.

FIGURE 1.4: *Homicide detectives investigate deaths that occur in different ways and locations.*

Investigations

Detectives are popular figures in movies and TV shows, where they can solve any case in two hours or less. The reality of police investigations is both more complex and interesting than shown on the screen. Investigators follow up cases documented by patrol officers, and while small departments might have one or two dedicated investigators responsible for all their cases, larger departments have the resources to train investigators for specific types of crimes. In the following sections, we'll discuss some, though not all, of those specialty areas.

Homicide

Death investigations (homicides) are the most serious cases that are undertaken by law enforcement. Homicide investigators examine a wide variety of death cases, ranging from accidents to murder.

In the event of a murder case, the defendant could be facing punishment up to and including the death penalty. The defense team will attack every aspect of the prosecution's case when representing their client. That means that the homicide team must prepare every case to withstand a skilled and thorough challenge at the trial.

Homicide investigators may also investigate industrial accidents, deaths that occur during medical procedures, and apparent natural deaths where there is no doctor to sign a death certificate. Attending autopsies and collecting evidence at the scene are also part of the homicide detective's duties.

Burglary

The crime of burglary is usually defined as "entering a building intending to commit a crime," usually theft. It is one of the most common crimes committed, and one of the least likely to be solved with an arrest. The reason it is so difficult to solve a burglary is that there are so seldom any witnesses; the homeowner simply returns from work or a vacation finding a door or window opened and items missing from his home. Commercial buildings and warehouses may be burglarized as well, with the criminals entering during non-business hours.

Burglary investigators start with relatively little material; there are seldom witnesses to a burglary, and physical evidence is often cleaned up by homeowners before police arrive. Some homeowners have video surveillance around their homes, since the cost of such equipment has come down over the last several years, but it is still fairly uncommon. Sometimes investigation is as easy as following a trail of footprints to a neighbor's house, but usually the investigators will find some partial fingerprints on the door or window at the point of entry. These partial prints may not be enough to identify the criminal out of a large pool of possible suspects, but they can be adequate to tie an individual criminal to the crime, or to confirm that one person was present at several scenes.

Burglars often steal in order to finance drug addictions, so they take items that are portable and easily sold. Good investigators develop relationships with pawnshops and other legitimate secondhand stores where criminals might try to sell the stolen items, and they know the laws of their state regarding the records such businesses are required to keep of their transactions.

Robbery

Robbery cases are different than burglary in that the theft occurs directly from a person, or in their presence, and it includes the use or threat of force to take property away. The theft of money from a gas station's cashier would be robbery if the cashier knew or believed the robber to be armed, or even if the robber simply threatened to beat the cashier if she did not cooperate. Because of the potential for violence, robbery is nearly always considered to be a more serious crime than burglary.

Robberies are usually committed by experienced, motivated criminals. Because they are often armed, the suspects pose a greater risk to the safety of officers during arrest and to witnesses who report the crimes. Fingerprints are not found as frequently at the scene of a robbery, but there is always at least one witness if the victim reported the crime. When suspects are identified and warrants are prepared, the robbery investigators work closely with operations units, such as SWAT or a specific high-risk warrant service team, to plan the arrest or search as safely as possible, while preserving the evidence sought.

Arson

Interestingly, many arson investigators are employed by fire departments rather than law enforcement agencies. Arson is the intentional burning of property, and it may be done to destroy evidence of other crimes, to victimize the property owner, or to fraudulently collect claim damages from an insurance company (sometimes by the property owner himself).

Though arson investigators follow all the same steps as other criminal investigators, their cases require specialized knowledge and experience. Arson investigators are trained to look for the clues that show where a fire started and how it spread. Accidental fires spread differently than intentional fires. The arson investigator interviews witnesses and firefighters as soon as possible, since the fire itself may destroy evidence of arson. Some clues to arson include the color of the flame and smoke, which might indicate chemicals (such as gasoline) used to start or accelerate the fire, or the condition of doors and windows, which may have been left open to allow more oxygen to reach the flames, or jammed closed to slow firefighting efforts.

Investigators also look into the victim's financial records to find hidden debts or any other need for money that might encourage the owner to set the fire. If the property is commercial, records of merchandise that should have been in the building will be compared with the debris found to verify that the merchandise was there when the property burned, and not stolen or removed beforehand.

Forgery

Forgery is the creation of a false document, or the alteration of a real document, in order to defraud someone. While this is usually a low-level crime involving an amateur criminal who changes the writing on a check, contract, or other document, it can be as serious as creating false currency or even works of art.

Forgery investigators work at all levels of law enforcement. The Secret Service is the federal agency responsible for enforcing forgery laws involving U.S. currency and government checks and other financial instruments. The FBI has had great success in breaking cases of art forgery, and Immigration and Customs Enforcement (ICE) is involved whenever these items are brought into the United States. Local agencies follow up on cases of check forging, but state agencies may be given the responsibility of investigating forged state lottery tickets, benefits checks or legal documents.

Juvenile Crime

In the U.S., the juvenile justice system is designed to divert youthful offenders from crime and reintegrate them into society before they become habitual criminals. This requires a different mindset and a more specialized knowledge of juvenile criminal topics and diversion resources than a typical patrol officer has. Investigators take into account not only the child's crime, but also his home life and family situation, to determine whether the young person should be removed from his environment.

Investigators work with court officers, probation, parents, school officials, and others in order to treat juveniles fairly and correctly. The goal is to avoid incarceration whenever appropriate. Sometimes this investigation helps the justice system to determine whether a juvenile should be tried as an adult; for example, if an investigation shows that the offender understood the nature of the crime he was committing.

Other Specialized Assignments

Detectives are also often assigned to positions investigating sex crimes, auto theft, trafficking in stolen property, drugs, vice crimes, and other specialized units.

Task Force Operations

State, local, and federal agencies often pool investigators with special skills for task force operations. These efforts might be directed toward a specific criminal who commits crimes across jurisdictions, or they might address multijurisdictional crimes, such as drug trafficking or terrorism.

Summary

Police work has always been challenging, and it is becoming increasingly technical and specialized. Each of the various law enforcement agencies has specific legal authority and responsibilities, and is accountable to the law as well as to the public it serves. This accountability is what keeps the police connected to the community, rather than becoming an impersonal arm of state power, as occurs in so many other countries.

As paramilitary organizations, police agencies use their rank structure and clear chains of command to assign duties to employees and ensure proper accountability within their departments. These chains of command can be expanded or contracted as needed for emergencies and events of various size and complexity; this enables an efficient response from the agencies involved. Using a standardized response plan, such as ICS, allows agencies from around the country to work together to mitigate large regional emergencies.

Each of the special units found in police agencies has a role to play in providing the safest community possible. A working officer, or a student, should aspire to become involved in the specialty that interests her most, but should always remember the basics of police work. As you continue to study law enforcement as a career, keep in mind the idea of public service and consider what that will mean to every officer, whether working patrol in a small rural department, or a specialized unit in a huge city or state agency.

Discussion Questions

1. The concept of decentralized government requires local control of as many governmental services as possible, including police services. In the U.S., this results in a myriad of police departments being used in many places. Do you think the use of these small departments increases accountability? Does it decrease efficiency?

2. The chain of command is an efficient means of transmitting information and orders, and it helps ensure that every member of an organization knows his or her responsibilities. What circumstances do you think would justify or necessitate communication outside the chain? When should an officer skip the sergeant and lieutenant and go directly to a captain? When should the captain communicate directly with an officer?

3. There are many more kinds of special units than are listed in this Module. What other types of units might your area need?

4. SWAT teams are used in extreme situations, and some people find their military equipment and aggressive tactics inappropriate for civilian police use. Do you think their use is ever appropriate? Can you think of a time you heard of a SWAT team used when the situation could have been better handled by regular police units? What are potential dangers of over reliance on tactical teams like SWAT?

5. Law enforcement agencies employ both are sworn police officers and unsworn technical and clerical staff. How much training in law and police procedure do you think the unsworn employees should have? How does the need for this training change when given to crime lab technicians, records clerks, or fingerprint examiners?

Key Terms

Accountability — Being liable or answerable for actions, progress, or success.

Chain of command — A series of ranks, positions, or job functions where each has authority over the personnel below.

Decentralized government — Concept where governmental services are provided and decisions made at the lowest possible level of government.

Incident Command System — The standardized emergency response planning framework designed to allow police, fire, and EMS units from anywhere in the U.S. to work together in a major emergency.

Incorporation — The act of creating a city or town as a corporate entity; gives a city or town the right to establish a local government.

Internal affairs unit — Police special unit tasked with investigating police corruption, brutality and other unprofessional actions.

Jurisdiction — The area or extent of law enforcement authority.

Municipal government — The government of a city or town.

Oversight committees — Group of people who are set up to provide watch over a police department's actions. Participants often include representatives of the community and police department.

Paramilitary — Group of people that operates like a military organization, with rank structure and chain of command.

Police department — The section of local government responsible for law enforcement.

Police special unit — Members of a police department specifically trained to handle specific, technical tasks.

Private police — Companies and individuals who are allowed by law to provide limited police services to paying customers; authority varies by state.

Sheriff — Elected law enforcement official at the county level.

Sheriff's department — The section of county government usually holding law enforcement responsibility in unincorporated areas of the county, particularly county buildings such as courts and jails.

Span of control — The number of employees a manager can effectively control.

State police — State agency department responsible for general law enforcement, often called a Highway Patrol.

MODULE 2
Applied Skills: Domestic Violence

Key Module Concepts:

- Definitions of domestic violence

- Problems associated with domestic violence calls

- An officer's responsibilities during domestic violence responses

- Gathering relevant information from participants in proper fashion

- Distinguishing between orders of protection

- Identifying the federal laws that protect the victim

Introduction

Responding to the scene of a possible domestic violence call can place officers in a very dangerous situation. Domestic disputes are often emotionally charged and can become highly volatile. When this type of dispute becomes a police matter, there is often a backlash from the participants against the authority who has arrived to provide security and keep the peace. However, intervention in domestic violence cases is critical to break what is often a cycle of destructive behavior and to prevent the escalation of violence. Protecting the innocent, prosecuting the guilty, and providing help for those in need are the goals of a domestic violence investigation. In this Module, we will examine the history, law, and response procedures for domestic violence cases.

Ask Yourself

- *What options does an officer have when diffusing a confrontation?*
- *What type of injuries should an officer look for when responding to a possible domestic violence call?*
- *What short- and long-term benefits are accomplished when law enforcement intervenes during domestic violence incidents?*

History Of Domestic Violence Investigations

Historically, law enforcement used the policy of discretion over duty to deal with domestic violence issues. Officers would often break up domestic disputes, threaten the parties with arrest if additional calls were received, then leave the scene. In many cases, officers would return to the same house many times to deal with ongoing domestic disputes; however, they did not intervene in any significant manner until someone was killed or sent to the hospital. Laws in the past tended to protect the sanctity of the home over the safety of the individuals within the home.

These attitudes about passive intervention were supported through local police training, as well as guidelines from the International Association of Chiefs of Police (IACP). Throughout the 1960s and '70s, the IACP advocated family or marriage counseling rather than making an arrest.

EXAMPLE:

In the 1970s, an officer received a radio dispatch to the scene of a domestic violence incident. As the officer approached the residence, he observed a male and female arguing and pushing each other on the front porch. The officer separated the couple and recommended that they contact a family services agency to help them work through their problems.

The officer's attitude was much like the majority of police departments in America: "This is not a police problem; it is a family problem." There was seldom a report written. However, there was a warning statement always given as the officer left the scene: "If I have to come back, I'll lock both of you up."

In the 1980s, laws were enacted and procedures were set in place that were directed toward protecting the victims of domestic violence. Today, police responses usually end up with an arrest.

A **pro-arrest policy**, where an arrest is required or preferred if the police officer finds probable cause that domestic battery has taken place, is the norm. This arrest takes place regardless of the victim's wishes in the matter. An arrest is made, social service support is engaged, and a detailed report is written.

Definitions Of Domestic Violence

Many definitions have been used in an attempt to categorize **domestic violence**, also known as domestic abuse. While domestic violence is of concern to both law enforcement and social service agencies, there is no universal term, description or classification used by all governmental jurisdictions.

For the purposes of law enforcement, the Department of Justice (DOJ) has provided the public with the following broad definitions for common domestic offenses:

– *Domestic violence* can be defined as a pattern of abusive behavior that is used by an intimate partner to gain or maintain power and control over the other intimate partner. Domestic violence can be physical, sexual, emotional, economic, or psychological actions or threats of actions that influence another person. This includes any behaviors that intimidate, manipulate, humiliate, isolate, frighten, terrorize, coerce, threaten, blame, hurt, injure, or wound someone. Domestic violence can be an issue in any of the following relationships (check your local state law):

- Spouse/former spouse
- Cohabitant/former cohabitant
- Dating relationship/former dating relationship
- Engagement relationship/former engagement relationship
- Co-parents of a child

- Child who is the subject of parental action
- People related by consanguinity or affinity within the second degree

– *Sexual assault* can be defined as any type of sexual contact or behavior that occurs by force or without consent of the recipient of the unwanted sexual activity. Falling under the definition of sexual assault is sexual activity, such as forced sexual intercourse, sodomy, child molestation, incest, fondling, and attempted rape. It also includes sexual acts against people who are unable to consent, either due to age or lack of capacity.

– *Dating violence* is defined as violence committed by a person who is or has been in a social relationship of a romantic or intimate nature with the victim. The existence of such a relationship shall be determined based on a consideration of the following factors:

- The length of the relationship
- The type of relationship
- The frequency of interaction between the persons involved in the relationship

– *Stalking* can be defined as a pattern of repeated and unwanted attention, harassment, contact, or any other conduct directed at an individual that would cause a reasonable person to feel fear

– *Criminal threats* are written or verbal statements that insinuate harm, even death, toward a victim and his/her loved ones, resulting in a reasonable fear of safety

– *Domestic disputes* are verbal or physical altercations between two or more people that require police intervention. The dispute is not required to progress past the verbal stage.

Resource - Crimes of violence against women are the largest category of calls made to police departments nationwide; they cost billions of dollars in medical expenses and productivity. While these numbers only reference American statistics, domestic violence is a global problem.

The United Nations Office on Drugs and Crime (UNODC) developed a handbook on "Effective Police Responses to Violence Against Women." While it is not intended to replace agency guidelines, the handbook is designed to explain to first responders how to investigate such a case.

The PDF of this handbook can be accessed at **http://www.unodc.org.**

Each state has domestic violence laws defined in the form of a criminal statute. That statute is what law enforcement uses to enforce domestic violence law.

The other element of domestic abuse relates to specific crimes associated with the situation. Most states document in specific statutes what crimes are considered domestic violence within that jurisdiction. These crimes may include the following:

- Assault
- Threats
- Stalking
- Criminal damage/vandalism
- Witness intimidation
- Sexual abuse
- Sexual assault
- Homicide
- Burglary
- Elder abuse
- Cruelty to animals

If the offense involves individuals in one of the previously described relationships, and the act that occurred constitutes one of the listed crimes covered by domestic violence law, then the case may constitute domestic violence.

Discretion and Non-Criminal Offenses

But when do family differences become classified as domestic violence? Does a mere argument constitute a crime?

Not all domestic differences constitute a crime or result in domestic violence. While a domestic difference may involve a disagreement, it does not necessarily constitute a police matter. If a situation escalates to threats or violence, then it may become a police matter.

As a police officer, it is important to understand what constitutes a domestic violence offense. A mere disagreement requires a different response than a criminal matter. In the case of domestic differences, the duty of an officer is to keep the peace and aid in conflict resolution; this usually does not require an arrest. However, detailed reports are typically submitted, carefully explaining in detail why further action was not taken.

Effectiveness Of An Arrest In Domestic Violence Cases

Treating domestic violence like a criminal violation, rather than strictly a civil or family matter, has produced many positive results. This was confirmed by a study documented by the Minneapolis Police Department in 1982. The city of Minneapolis was divided into three distinct areas. Three options were given to the officers responsible for answering domestic disturbance calls. The officers were instructed to use only the following three options, if possible.

Option 1	Option 2	Option 3
Attempt to diffuse the situation with no further conflict, and refer the participants to counseling services	Calm the situation by instructing one of the parties involved to leave the house for a few hours (or overnight), with the hope that the situation would resolve itself through time and distance without further police involvement	Make an arrest if sufficient probable cause is evident, thereby strictly enforcing the criminal code and effectively ending the conflict by placing the suspect in jail

FIGURE 2.1: *The options available to Minneapolis police officers answering domestic disturbance calls during a 1982 study.*

The Minneapolis Police tracked each family and gathered follow-up information anonymously to see which option reduced violence in the home and reduced calls to police. In the end, the information showed that domestic violence decreased in many of the homes where an arrest was made.

Interestingly, statistics found that over 30 percent of the time, officers would have to respond multiple times to the same scene for another domestic violence incident between the parties involved. Over 40 percent of those parties involved in a domestic dispute in which one party left the scene had to have the police return within a few hours. However, approximately only 10 percent of those arrested were involved in another domestic disturbance with the same person, requiring the police to return.

This study suggests that a lawful arrest of a person involved in a domestic disturbance has a positive effect on the number of repeat calls from a residence.

Domestic Violence Facts and Myths

Domestic violence is not just a concern of the participants and victims; it affects society as a whole.

Innocent children who witness, or are victims of, violence that occurs without consequences may adopt the behavior as acceptable. This **intergenerational chain of violence** not only models the child's perception of anger management, but also furthers the acceptability of hostile acts in the future. This fact alone demonstrates the profound importance of police officers breaking the cycle of violence. Below is a chart reflecting the positive impact of law enforcement intervention in domestic violence cases.

	Batterer	**Victim**	**Child**
Positive Impact	Understands that this degree of abuse is a criminal behavior that will not be permitted Experiences the negative results through arrests, fines, criminal records, or jail time May cease violent behavior	Grasps the knowledge of civil liberties Recovers control that was lost in the relationship Reduces guilt and shame Becomes less likely to repeat a series of violent associations May advocate for other victims turned survivors	Comprehends that violence is illegal Avoids continuing the abuse Learns that the aggressor is held liable and not the victim and/or self May become a voice for others

FIGURE 2.2: *The table demonstrates the positive impact of law enforcement intervention in domestic violence incidents.*

Some ideas about domestic violence are based on misconceptions and myths that have been in place for many years, including:

- Domestic violence involves a momentary loss of temper
- Domestic violence is a private matter
- Domestic violence only happens in poor or uneducated families
- If the spouse stays in a abusive household, then that person deserves what she (or he) gets
- If the spouse really wanted to leave an abusive relationship, then that person would move out
- Fighting is normal in domestic life
- Wives don't batter husbands

These myths are countered by documented facts concerning domestic violence. The homicide rate statistics around domestic violence are particularly alarming:

- Family violence accounted for 11% of all reported and unreported violence between 1998 and 2002
- About 22% of murders in 2002 were committed by family members
- Of the nearly 500,000 men and women in state prisons for a violent crime in 1997, 15% were there for a violent crime against a family member

Source: Bureau of Justice Statistics – U.S. Department of Justice

The methods of abuse may vary, but typically an abuser, or **batterer**, uses force and intimidation to gain power and control in one of these ways:

- Emotional abuse
- Isolation
- Minimizing, denying and blaming
- Using children
- Economic abuse
- Coercion and threats

FIGURE 2.3: *To ensure the safety of everyone involved, including law enforcement officers, certain guidelines should be followed when responding to domestic violence calls.*

Some forms of abuse are not as easy to recognize as an assault or damage to property. Recognizing and understanding these facts enables officers to deal more effectively with the complexities of handling domestic violence cases.

Responding To Domestic Violence Calls

An effective and safe response to domestic violence calls requires following procedure and strong officer safety tactics. About 8% of the officers killed in the line of duty between 2000-2009 were responding to domestic violence calls. In 2009 alone, 33% of officers assaulted in the line of duty were responding to disturbance calls, including domestic disputes, according to the FBI Uniform Crime Report. Following the safety tactics listed below can protect an officer from the negative consequences of responding to such calls.

Upon receiving a dispatch to a domestic violence situation, the officer should first establish and confirm the address. If the address is confirmed, most police records departments can provide the officer with a "call history," or a list of events that transpired if and when police were sent to this location before. If this is not automatically provided, it should be requested. Knowing what others have previously found at a given location can be helpful. For example, knowing that an officer had seized a firearm on a previous call could provide a safety advantage for the officer currently handling the situation.

If possible, the officer should try to identify the names of the parties involved and find out their history with law enforcement. Information on prior arrest records, convictions, or associations with gangs or drugs could enable the responder to quickly assess the circumstances of the call upon arrival.

The officer should never park a police vehicle immediately in front of the residence. Instead, the officer should quietly park a short distance away and approach the home on foot. This will give the officer the opportunity to listen to what is going on before making contact, and perhaps even observe what is transpiring from a surveillance position. The officer could also use this surveillance time to determine the nature of the dispute and the number of people involved. This information should be relayed to the dispatcher and any other responding units immediately. If possible, when speaking to the dispatcher, the officer should try to identify the level of aggression involved, if any weapons are present, and how much backup might be required.

Once the decision to make contact is made, the officer should make a tactical entry. Typically, this means the officer stands at the side of the door when knocking (instead of directly in front of it), and announces his presence.

Once entry is secured, the officer should scan for weapons and gain control of the scene. Locating and separating occupants and participants, scanning for and securing any weapons, and checking for any medical emergencies are all high priority tasks. There are many variables involved in making the decision of what to do first, such as the size of the residence, the number of people involved, the degree of aggression, and the number of officers on site, but safety should be the foremost concern.

If a suspect is quickly identified, or a threatening or disruptive person engages an officer, that person should be removed from the immediate area and secured. The officer should attempt to calm all parties; ideally, they will be cooperative, but this will not always be the case.

The officer should always try to identify the aggressor. There are several methods that are useful in making this identification.

- Determine who is in fear of whom
- Identify who poses the most danger to others
- Note whether one party has a violent history
- Find indications of self-defense
- Use witness statements to support either account

Aggressors may be identified by other indicators, including:

- Prior arrest(s) for domestic violence
- Prior conviction(s) for assault or violent crime
- History of substance abuse
- History of mental illness
- Weapons in their possession or control
- Threats or threatening body language in the officer's presence
- History of stalking
- Suicide attempts or threats in the past, or in the officer's presence

The officer should make note of any spontaneous statements that are made, such as a suspect saying, "I didn't hit you hard enough for you to call the cops," or "Why did you call the police?" These types of comments may indicate who called the police or who the aggressor was, and should be included in the subsequent report.

All parties should be separated out of each other's earshot to prevent them from influencing each other's statements or falsely collaborating each other's stories. Maintaining calm and civility is important to prevent emotional disruptions that could cause an officer to miss relevant information. The officer should allow the participants to speak with little to no interruptions, and then follow up with specific questions to determine the facts of the situation.

Officers can utilize the following as a checklist for managing the participants:

- Separate parties so one person's responses do not influence the other party
- Keep an eye on all the individuals present to ensure everyone's safety, including law enforcement personnel

Officers should note all injuries or property damage, take photographs, and carefully document everything in the report. They must also get written statements and interview all witnesses during the investigation. All injuries, whether offensive or defensive, should be documented. An injured participant is encouraged by officers to seek medical attention, but cannot be forced to do so. If this happens, the officer should document the refusal of such service.

The officer may determine that no crime was committed and the situation amounted to a mere family disagreement. In this case, a detailed report outlining all the factors leading to this conclusion must be completed. Another outcome might be the arrest of one or more parties involved if a crime were committed.

Other actions might include advising the victim to obtain a temporary restraining order or an emergency order of protection. These court orders have different names in various jurisdictions. Officers may also refer victims to social service agencies, which can play a critical role in the support of the victim after the scene is secured.

Documenting The Criminal Act

There are several important factors to note when writing case reports, including:

- Signs the batterer was under the influence of alcohol and/or controlled substances
- Previous response calls to the same address involving the same parties (abuser and victim)
- Notation of any firearms or deadly weapons found at the scene, as well as seizure of any weaponry (describe the model, the location, and if it had been used)
- Any injuries or damage to property
- Detailed witness statements

Injuries are a likely consequence of these types of calls. Officers should note if the individual's wounds are offensive or defensive. Offensive injuries on a victim occur when the aggressor attacks; offensive injuries may be found on an aggressor when the victim protects him/herself from attack. Defensive injuries are located on a victim who was acting in self-defense, or may be inflicted on an attacker as a result of the victim's attempts to defend him/herself. Examples of each type of injury are listed in Figure 2.4.

	Offensive Injuries to Victim	Offensive Injuries to Attacker	Defensive Injuries to Victim	Defensive Injuries to Attacker
Source of Injury	Injuries are inflicted by the attacker as a direct result of the attack	Injuries are inflicted by the actions against the victim	Injuries sustained to the victim while attempting to defend or protect him/herself	Injuries sustained by the attacker when defending him/herself from the victim's retaliation
Examples	Scratches Bone fractures or breaks Bruising	Injury to the knuckles after punching the victim Injuries to foot after kicking the victim	Bruises on the back from laying in the fetal position in a posture of self-defense Injuries to the hands from blocking slaps or punches	Scratches inflicted by a victim to the attacker's face while trying to get out of a stranglehold Bite marks to the attacker's hands in an attempt by the victim to keep his/her mouth uncovered

FIGURE 2.4: *Explanation of offensive and defensive injuries by affected party.*

Photographs can help support a domestic violence case. Photographs included with the police report should document the crime scene and injuries to the various parties, even those that are not presently visible. It is a good practice to take additional photos of the injuries 24 hours after the event, when bruises become visible. Sometimes the victim(s) cannot appear in court; any pictures of the abused person's injuries may be submitted in his or her absence.

Officers should also photograph any damaged property or unusual conditions on the premises, such as overturned furniture. The state of cleanliness and neatness of the residence should also be documented.

If the information can be obtained, the report should include the **course of conduct**, or the pattern and series of violent acts that have been enabled over a given length of time (however long or short) with a continuing sense of purpose.

Common Services Providing Protection

There are a variety of support systems available to victims of domestic violence, ranging from court-ordered protection orders to social service agency support. Officers cannot assume that the victim knows what to do after the aggressor is arrested or other disposition of the case is made. This information should be furnished, and guidance should be provided at the scene to any victims involved in the case.

Orders of Protection

Courts have the ability to issue orders of protections and injunctive orders, which are valuable tools used to protect victims of domestic violence.

Prior to issuing a protective order, the initial petition must be heard in a family or civil court hearing. If there is a threat of immediate violence or violence has already occurred, the court has the option of authorizing an order of protection, sometimes called a restraining order, a civil action which has criminal penalties that can be enforced by the police. The order of protection may be issued in the absence of the offending party. A hearing such as this, which takes place with one of the relevant parties missing, is known in legal terminology as an ***ex parte* hearing**.

Once the order of protection is issued, certain guidelines are set for all parties involved. The court does its best to produce regulations that establish a legal barrier between the victim and the batterer. When one of these protective orders is violated, police have the authority to intervene by shielding the innocent and arresting the guilty.

EXAMPLE:
Jane has petitioned the court for an order of protection from her husband John, who has physically struck and verbally threatened her numerous times. One of the conditions set by the judge is that

no communication shall exist between the couple. John continues to contact her, making threatening statements to Jane via email and instant messaging services. Jane saves and prints copies of what John has written by date and time, calls the police, and has John arrested for violating the order of protection.

As a police officer, it is important to know the differences among the types of restraining orders.

- **Emergency protective order (EPO):** An order that is requested by the responding officer on behalf of the defending party (or sometimes from the party himself) that offers instant, yet limited, protection

- **Domestic violence temporary restraining order (DVTRO):** An order that is requested by the victim without prior court notice. DVTROs are often issued the same day they are requested and remain in effect until the scheduled review hearing. Both parties will then have the opportunity to explain why a permanent restraining order should or should not be issued.

- ***Ex Parte* temporary restraining order:** An order that is requested by the victim in a civil action. No prior notice or hearing is necessary.

- **Order to show cause (OSC):** A hearing is held to determine if the Ex Parte Temporary Restraining Order is warranted and needs to be extended

- **Order after hearing (OAH):** An order that is enforced up to five years. This is issued at the OSC hearing.

The court may grant a permanent injunction with no expiration date after a full trial on the merits of a case has been conducted.

Federal Protection for Victims

The Office on Violence Against Women (OVM) was created in 1995 as a permanent division of the Department of Justice. The Director is appointed by the President and confirmed by the Senate. The **Violence Against Women Act** (VAWA) of 1994 falls under the jurisdiction of OVM.

Congress passed VAWA in acknowledgement of the severity of crimes against women. VAWA was enacted in an effort to show that Congress was actively working to improve protection to those who were abused or involved in domestic violence situations. It was also an effort to show that all levels of government are taking domestic violence seriously. OVM has been awarded more than $3 billion to work with state, local, and tribal government agencies.

The VAWA 2000 reauthorization strengthened the original VAWA to protect immigrants who were victims of domestic violence and dating violence. The VAWA was reauthorized again in 2005 to cover existing loopholes and further reinforce the act by providing greater access to those populations that may have been underserved.

Resource - Unfortunately, there are a number of officers who find themselves on the wrong side of domestic violence. In fact, domestic violence within a police household is two to four times more common than in the general population. What makes the situation even more disturbing is that these trained men and women know how to be intimidating and how to use different forms of weaponry. They know how to bend the law in their favor, sometimes even convincing colleagues to stalk the victim.

Purple Berets is a grassroots organization dedicated to the rights of those who have been abused through domestic violence. The Web site even offers helpful information for those who are trapped in a situation when their loved one is both a cop and batterer.

For more information, go to **http://www.purpleberets.org.**

Summary

It is important to take a look at the evolutionary changes in how law enforcement tackles the problem of domestic violence. Before, the archetypical response of the police was generally, at most, an informal comment that the individuals involved needed to seek counseling.

Domestic disputes can be the most deadly situations that police officers encounter. Regardless of the course of action taken at the conclusion of the domestic violence incident, there are certain precautions officers must take to protect themselves and those involved. Upon arrival, the responding officer should wait for backup. After another officer arrives on the scene, the officers can make contact with the people involved.

The immediate safety of the victim(s) involved is of the utmost concern in any domestic violence scenario. To ensure safety, the officer must provide some type of lasting resolution. As a part of the many duties a police officer has, documenting the domestic incident is vital. By recording those persons involved separately, it ensures that the aggressor does not influence the story of the victim. Any documentation — written and photographed — may be used in a court case.

Those who have been injured may require protection to overcome the traumatic experience. Both victims and officers may request a restraining order to legally bar an abusive person from making contact with the abused party. If an order has been violated, law enforcement has the authority to act responsibly. Definitions of domestic violence may vary across the country, but the end result is the same: a person, male or female, suffers the humiliation of verbal or physical abuse in some form or manner.

Discussion Questions

1. Describe the manner and attitude of police officers' handling of domestic violence incidents in the past. What was the general pattern of handling these investigations?

2. Illustrate how domestic violence calls are handled today by law enforcement agencies. In your opinion, which method seems to be the most effective? Why?

3. Explain the three options used by the Minneapolis Police Department Study in determining how to treat domestic violence issues. How were their methods different from how types of cases were handled in the past?

4. What are some of the problems associated with a police response to domestic violence calls?

5. What criteria should a police officer use to determine how the responses should be handled in a criminal or conflict matter?

6. Explain the history of the Violence Against Women Act of 1994 (VAWA) and give reasons for later updates to VAWA.

Key Terms

Accountability — Being liable or answerable for actions, progress, or success.

Batterer — A person who uses force against another to induce fear or physical harm.

Course of conduct — A pattern of behavior or occurrences over any given period of time.

Criminal threat — A statement, either verbal or written, insinuating harm or even death toward the victim and/or loved ones, resulting in a reasonable fear for safety.

Dating violence — Violence committed by a person who is or has been in a social relationship of a romantic or intimate nature with the victim; the relationship is established based on the length and type and frequency of interaction between the parties.

Defensive injuries — The injuries sustained by the victim while trying to shield him/herself from the aggressor's attacks; defensive injuries may also be inflicted on the aggressor by the victim while he/she actively retaliates against an attack.

Domestic dispute — A verbal or physical altercation between two or more people that requires police intervention; the dispute may or may not have progressed to a physical attack.

Domestic violence — A pattern of physically, sexually, and/or emotionally abusive behaviors used by one individual to assert power or maintain control toward an intimate partner (current or former) or family member. Also referred to as domestic abuse.

Domestic violence temporary restraining order (DVTRO) — A temporary order of protection resulting from an alleged domestic incident, put in place while a permanent order is decided or dismissed. This order may be issued in an *ex parte* hearing.

***Ex parte* hearing** — A hearing held before the court by one party in the absence of, or without giving notice to, the other party.

Intergenerational chain of violence — A cycle during which a child witnesses continuous domestic violence and the batterer suffers no consequences. The child believes this is acceptable behavior. There is a greater risk of violent behavior perpetuating in later generations.

Offensive injuries — The injuries an aggressor inflicts on a victim; also injuries an aggressor obtains while the victim is protecting himself or herself during conflict.

Order after hearing (OAH) — An order issued at the order to show cause hearing that can be enforced for up to five years.

Order of protection — A court order that prohibits a person from having any type of contact with the victim; a restraining order.

Order to show cause (OSC) — A court order that requires one or more parties involved in a trial to explain or prove something to the court; frequently used to provide a judge with additional information to facilitate a decision on another order or motion.

Pro-arrest policy — An arrest is recommended if the police officer has probable cause to believe that a domestic battery has taken place, with a written report documenting the reasons no arrest took place.

Sexual assault — Any type of sexual contact or behavior that occurs by force or without consent of the recipient of the unwanted sexual activity. Includes forced sexual intercourse, sodomy, child molestation, incest, fondling, and attempted rape. It also includes sexual acts against people who are unable to consent either due to age or lack of capacity.

Violence Against Women Act (VAWA) — U.S. federal law that provides services and protection for women who are victims of domestic violence.

MODULE 3

Crowd Control & Chemical Agents

Key Module Concepts:

- The primary objective of crowd control

- Various riot control formations used by law enforcement

- Thr range of procedures for controlling potentially dangerous crowds

- The three most commonly used chemical agents in U.S. law enforcement

- Different methods for deploying chemical agents in a civil disobedience situation

- Proper decontamination process after exposure to chemical agents used in law enforcement

Introduction

In the United States, people have the Constitutional right to **free assembly,** or to gather to collectively express, promote, pursue and/or defend common interests. Law enforcement officers are required to preserve this right and actively protect people who choose to exercise it reasonably, but law enforcement also has the responsibility of keeping the peace and protecting the public. Law enforcement officers must be prepared to deal with public gatherings, ranging from simple peaceful assemblies of people attending a sporting event to emotionally charged political demonstrations that have the potential to evolve quickly into a riot.

Crowd control often requires coordination and cooperation between private security and public law enforcement officers. Security professionals often provide unique insight to crowd control management situations. Large venues and entertainment companies hire private sector experts who specialize in crowd management and emergency response. Law enforcement officers must be able to maintain order when crowds form, and be prepared to disperse or control crowds that become unruly. The ability to control crowds effectively and maintain a safe environment hinges on the understanding of crowd behavior, effective response procedures and policies, and knowledge of the laws that apply to free assembly.

Module Three addresses crowd control and a variety of techniques that can be used for dispersing both hostile and non-hostile groups of people. Additionally, an in-depth look into the use, deployment, and treatment for common law enforcement chemical agents is provided.

Ask Yourself

How does the First Amendment of the United States Constitution affect the way U.S. law enforcement is required to handle crowds?

- *What makes a crowd potentially dangerous?*
- *How can law enforcement maintain order while protecting citizens' First Amendment rights?*
- *How have U.S. law enforcement tactics and techniques for dealing with crowds changed over the past 50 years? How does this relate to the First Amendment?*

Crowd Control

Law enforcement has long been charged with crowd control, though their methods have not always met with public approval, particularly as it relates to civil disobedience.

Civil disobedience is the refusal to obey certain laws or rules as a means of forcing concessions from the government. The way that law enforcement has dealt with crowds engaged in civil disobedience has changed substantially since the 1960s and 1970s, when public protests in the U.S. frequently turned into riots. Hard-line and undisciplined response tactics used by police during that period sometimes resulted in an escalation of crowd violence rather than effectively facilitating crowd control. News reports often focused negatively on the response of law enforcement to violent protests. This led to a decline in public opinion of how law enforcement responded to crowd control situations.

Today, while the fundamentals of crowd control tactics are largely the same, the way law enforcement officers implement these tactics has changed greatly. Additionally, law enforcement has taken a more proactive approach to managing crowds before events occur.

It is important to recognize that not all crowd situations involve civil disobedience, and that it is a police officer's responsibility to protect both an individual's right of free speech and right of assembly. It is also a police officer's responsibility to protect the lives and the property of all people. Therefore, law enforcement officers must be able to discern the difference between a legal protest and a situation where a crowd has begun to violate the rights of others.

Riots never happen spontaneously. Crowds develop in phases, and at each phase a crowd may behave differently. Law enforcement must be able to adjust its actions and responses to the crowd as this happens. In order to do this, it is essential that police officers understand the tactical principles required to control crowds, all while protecting the First Amendment rights of the crowd and providing safety for the entire community.

What's That Term?

*A **riot** is defined as a disturbance of the public peace by three or more persons who have assembled with a common intent. The Rodney King uprising in Los Angeles (1992) is an example of a famous American riot.*

Types of Crowds

Law enforcement and security have identified several types of crowds. Although all of these crowds can assemble peacefully and lawfully, they require police and security awareness, as they can rapidly change to violent situations. For general purposes of identification, the following terms distinguish the crowd types law enforcement officers may encounter:

- **Casual crowds:** These are groups that happen to be present at a given place but are not unified or organized. They don't have a leader or purpose; individual interests motivate the participants. An example of a casual crowd would be a group of teens hanging out in a mall parking lot.

- **Cohesive crowds:** These groups have a specific purpose for being together, such as a sporting event or entertainment event. They have a common interest but not a common purpose.

- **Expressive crowds:** The people in an expressive crowd are held together by a common goal; they share similar attitudes about a given topic. They often have well defined leadership. They typically have a unified mood, and their intentions are fairly clear. Examples may include political rallies or picket lines.

• **Aggressive crowds:** This type of crowd has strong emotions, clear leadership, and is engaged in aggressive action. They have intentionally come together for a highly emotional event and may become destructive. These crowds are the most difficult to control because they are focused, determined, and motivated to defy and confront authority.

By having a common frame of reference for describing crowds, the officers, security personnel, and commanders can understand a situation quickly and plan a response accordingly.

FIGURE 3.1: *Different types of crowds call for different methods of police response.*

How to Prevent Disorder

Law enforcement engages in numerous proactive crowd management activities; these often begin with the intelligence function. By being aware of future events at which potentially unruly crowds can gather, law enforcement can prepare to limit the risks of public disorder in advance. Understanding how crowds gather, think, and operate can also help prevent unruly gatherings from escalating into a riot.

Intelligence information pertaining to crowd control, from advanced knowledge of entertainment, political, and sporting events to subversive activities involving radical groups, historically violent protesters, and criminal street gangs, can help law enforcement prepare plans to prevent or mitigate unruly crowds. For example, if a concert is scheduled at a popular club and intelligence reports indicate that rival gang members are planning a confrontation there, crowd control experts can plan traffic flow in a way that might preclude someone from carrying out a drive-by shooting. If rival political groups are scheduling protests that may result in violent confrontations, the police can schedule adequate security, set up barricades, and organize the area in a way to minimize face-to-face contact between the groups, all while allowing them to protest peacefully.

Intelligence can also help identify leaders of groups and outside agitators who have come to cause a disturbance. Law enforcement personnel can work with responsible group leaders to ensure a successful and safe public gathering. The police can also plan to monitor known crowd agitators so they can be arrested quickly and removed from the area if they break the law.

When preplanning a response, it is imperative to organize a "safety-valve," or route enabling people to leave quickly if the crowd becomes disruptive. If a crowd becomes hostile, some of the people gathered may want to leave rather than be caught in a dangerous situation. If they are trapped in a mob, they become part of the problem. If they can be quickly moved out of the area, the number of people to be managed is greatly reduced. Preplanning an escape route for attendees, keeping exits open, and maintaining the flow of traffic out of the area are just a few steps that can be taken in advance of a public gathering.

Information about weapons and potential for violence is also critical intelligence information that should be passed on to police and security personnel assigned to a crowd response. This pre-incident information and preparation can help the first responders to safely and effectively protect the public.

Procedures for Controlling Potentially Dangerous Crowds

Procedures for controlling potentially dangerous crowds can vary, depending on whether the gathering of people is lawful or unlawful, or if the event is planned or spontaneous. Lawful events such as rallies, marches, parades, sporting events, labor disputes, parties, disasters, entertainment events, political events, or community celebrations all have the potential to evolve into demonstrations, protests, sit-ins, and other forms of civil disobedience up to and including riots.

Dealing with these types of events requires close coordination between law enforcement, security, and other organizations to reduce the chance that lawful gatherings will turn into unlawful or riot situations.

Whenever a law enforcement agency is made aware of an event that will draw a crowd, attempts should be made by the agency to establish communication and a liaison with the involved groups. Working with the involved groups ahead of time to establish clear guidelines and rules for the gathering that are lawful can defuse problems before they arise. Explaining to the group leadership that law enforcement is available to help protect their rights, but that unlawful acts will not be tolerated, can help to establish rapport with the group leadership that might be needed at another time.

A clear command structure should be established before the event, and if time permits, additional training should be afforded to all officers that will be assigned to the event. Law enforcement leadership should make initial assessments, and continual assessments should be made throughout the course of the entire event.

If unlawful acts begin to take place, it is essential to recognize whether they are the acts of individuals or indications of an upcoming riot. The use of crowd control tactics and formations should be used to apprehend anyone acting unlawfully.

Regardless of the behavior of the crowd, law enforcement officers should act professionally. The potential for hostility or unlawful acts does not equate to unlawful acts being committed. Until unlawful acts are committed, a professional demeanor and attitude toward the crowd can help to deescalate the situation and encourage event attendees to remain lawful.

Once the event is over, it is important that post-event reports are conducted, and the findings are disseminated among law enforcement leadership. Lessons learned, whether positive or negative, would be useful when planning the response to the next event that contains a potentially dangerous crowd.

Methods for Non-Hostile Crowd Dispersal

The First Amendment of the United States Constitution provides that people are allowed to speak freely and assemble, and law enforcement officers must be able to discern the difference between a

FIGURE 3.2: *Even peaceful gatherings may require law enforcement intervention.*

lawful gathering and a crowd that is committing unlawful acts. Hostile acts are not the only unlawful actions that a crowd can take that would require law enforcement to disperse it. Citizens and businesses not participating in the gathering have the right to continue their normal business and activities freely, without concern for safety or security. Protection under the First Amendment does not mean that a crowd has the right to infringe or abuse the civil or property rights of others. In the event that a crowd violates the rights of others, even through non-hostile acts, law enforcement has a duty to disperse the crowd and restore order.

It is always desirable to avoid situations that require physical police intervention, especially when the crowd has not yet become hostile or violent. A variety of techniques and tactics may be attempted to resolve a non-hostile civil disobedience situation before physical force is utilized. While it is not required that police officers use the least intrusive force option to regain control, it is imperative that they use the minimum force that is reasonable under the circumstances.

One of the most common tools used by law enforcement to deal with non-hostile crowds is the use of simple dispersal orders, which should be specific to the situation, should be professionally delivered, and should incorporate the following elements:

- The agency requiring dispersal
- A statement that the event has been declared an unlawful activity
- A statement that all persons in the immediate area are required to disperse immediately or will be arrested
- Routes for dispersal and a specific time frame allowed for dispersal

Dispersal orders should be delivered in such a manner that individuals in the crowd can be reasonably expected to be aware of them. There are a number of ways this can be accomplished. Written notices can be handed out; use of amplified sound or bullhorns can be used; loud speech, postings or signs, or a combination of all of these, can be effective.

When using dispersal orders, officers should be positioned around the crowd and use video or audio taping whenever possible to show that the order was given and the group reasonably could know of it. The order should be given at least twice, if possible, before officers are allowed to move into the crowd or make arrests.

CASE STUDY

Imagine arriving at the scene of a non-violent demonstration, where a large group of environmentalists have conducted a sit-down on the headquarters property of a local logging firm. Patrol officers initially responded at the request of the company, but quickly realized they lacked the manpower to remove a group of over 500 people without a major incident. A crowd control team was then requested. By the time your squad arrives at the scene, the protestors have been on the property for over two hours. Members of the logging company's management team are visibly frustrated at their inability to conduct work in their normal fashion. The crowd refuses to leave the property or allow the company's trucks and equipment to leave the property; and the group organizers have begun leading the rest of the group in a chant that proclaims they will not leave the property until the company agrees to stop cutting down rain forests in South America. The local media has made it to the scene as well.

While the crowd has not become violent, it is apparent that their actions have violated the rights of others, that tempers are beginning to flare both within the group and within the company's management team, and that a mob mentality is rising. The protest group is also in violation of a variety of municipal codes, and according to state law, it has committed the act of criminal trespass.

How did things go wrong in this situation? Based on the information provided, what steps could have been taken by protestors in order to keep their event lawful? Knowing that it took the protestors considerable time to plan and execute an event like this, what steps could law enforcement have taken prior to the event, or during the initial phases of the event, to help keep the crowd's activities lawful? Even though it is apparent that law enforcement has probable cause to begin making arrests, is that wholly necessary at this point based on the information provided? What alternatives are available?

Crowd Control for First Responders

The first officer at the scene of a disturbance that may become a crowd control situation must take several immediate steps. The first step is to move into a safe position of observation and request backup. While awaiting backup, the first responder should monitor crowd actions and assess the size of the crowd, what their agenda appears to be, and the age of the participants. A crowd of 30 young teenagers at a mall will be handled differently than an older crowd of 200 angry rioters. The first responder should be on the lookout for weapons among participants. Initial steps should also include identifying crowd leaders. The information gathered must be relayed to command and dispatch.

When backup arrives, options for officers might include establishing a rapport with crowd leaders and directing the crowd to disperse. Officers should be polite but firm, and should always remain impartial. Initiating physical contact with a crowd by pushing or shoving participants may result in the level of tensions escalating. If a crowd has the potential to become dangerous, officers might remove or isolate the leaders and try to break the crowd into small groups. Use of force should be avoided, if possible.

The three principles of riot control involve containment: keeping the crowd from growing, keeping the crowd isolated from others, and working toward dispersal of the crowd.

Crowd Control Formations

The use of squad **crowd control formations** offers a practical method of delivering a controlled tactical response in order to contain riots. When properly deployed, squad formations can allow law enforcement to quickly escalate or deescalate their actions and reactions based on the crowd's activities. The mere appearance of a competent, well organized, and professional group of police officers in a squad formation has the ability to cause a disorderly group to cease disruptive or unlawful activities.

Crowd control formations rely on teamwork. Unit integrity is essential for the team, and each officer must exercise personal discipline to ensure that the team integrity is maintained. Independent actions have the ability to jeopardize the work of the team and place all officers within the formation in danger.

The number of officers assigned to a squad can vary substantially, depending on a number of factors. Some factors include the mission of the crowd, the size of the crowd that needs to be controlled, the location of the crowd, and the assets available to the law enforcement agency. Regardless of size, the squad element typically contains four primary positions, each with its own distinct responsibilities. These are the squad leader, the point officer, team leaders, and squad members.

Ask Yourself

Crowd control formations offer a much better option to law enforcement in a riot situation than having to resort directly to lethal force. However, proper training in formations is required. Transitioning between formations and conducting arrests and rescues while facing a hostile crowd is difficult at best. Agencies should provide officers with specialized riot control training prior to deploying them to a riot or crowd control situation. Based on what you know of the structure of law enforcement agencies, what organizations do you think would be well versed in crowd control and riot formations?

Squad Positions

Squad leaders report directly to the tactical commander. The squad leader will give all orders related to assembly, formation, and movement of the squad, and assign the remaining members of the formation as the point officer, team leaders or squad members. Squad leaders often are positioned behind the formation; they provide directions and commands to the squad from this position, all while monitoring the activity of the squad and the crowd.

FIGURE 3.3: *Officers assigned to public gatherings must be properly trained in crowd control methods.*

The **point officer** is typically placed at the front and center in most crowd control formations, and usually has first contact with the crowd. The point officer is appointed as the second in command of a crowd control formation, and he reports directly to the squad leader. Other squad members determine their positions based on the position taken by the point officer.

Team leaders receive their direction directly from the squad leader. They are typically senior officers within the squad, and are often placed in charge of any special weapons or tools assigned to the squad, such as chemical agents or less lethal weapons systems.

The remainder of the squad is made up of squad members. **Squad members** receive their orders from their assigned team leader and make up the bulk of the formation.

Formation Types

The tactical commander or the officer in charge of the scene usually chooses the type of formation used in a crowd control situation. When selecting the appropriate formation, factors that must be considered, include:

- The size, demeanor, attitude and intent of the crowd
- Terrain
- Availability of dispersal routes
- The objectives of the department
- The number of officers available
- The training and experience of the officers
- Available equipment and resources

There are a number of basic squad formations that have been proven successful in crowd control and riot situations. The most common formations include the column formation, the skirmish line, the arrest/rescue formation, the diagonal formation, and the wedge formation. While there are several variations of these basic formations in use by different U.S. law enforcement agencies, these five represent the foundation that most other formations are built from.

Almost all formations in crowd control can originate as the **column formation**, which is normally used to move a squad from one location to another, to divide a crowd, or as a lead-in to other formations. The column allows the squad leader to easily maintain discipline while his squad is en route to the actual crowd or riot location, and promotes the confidence of the individual squad members. It is very easy to maintain, and its appearance can be intimidating to the crowd. To form a column formation, officers simply line up one behind the other. Normally, the squad leader will take up a position near the middle of the column in order to facilitate better command and control, and then will evenly distribute his team leaders to the front and rear to help with communication.

A **skirmish line** looks very similar to a column formation, but it moves very differently and is used for different reasons. Skirmish lines are traditionally used to move small crowds in a specific direction, to block access to restricted areas, or to contain a group within a specific area. They are especially easy to form from a column formation and can easily be supplemented with additional columns. To form a skirmish line, officers simply stand shoulder to shoulder in a straight line.

Whenever a rescue is needed or officers need to affect an arrest in the middle of a hostile crowd, an **arrest/rescue formation** is used. The arrest/rescue formation forms a dynamic perimeter within the hostile environment by having officers form a circle around a designated group or individual while facing outward. This affords the officers protection while conducting the rescue or affecting the arrest within the circle protection, keeping the rest of the crowd at bay. However, it is very difficult to transition into and out of the arrest/rescue formation; it lacks significant mobility because it requires some of the officers in the formation to move sideways and backwards as the formation moves.

The **diagonal formation** is sometimes referred to as an echelon formation. Similar to the column, the diagonal formation uses a slanted line of officers to clear crowds from the side of a building or wall, or to change the direction of a crowd. It can also be used to force groups of people into side streets or into open areas as needed. A hazard of the diagonal formation is that it is easier for crowd members to get behind than other formations. Additional squads or formations may be required as backup to prevent this from happening while the diagonal formation moves the crowd.

While difficult to maintain and move laterally, the **wedge formation** is highly effective at breaking crowds into smaller segments and clearing intersections. It is also very effective for penetrating a crowd for short distances. The wedge can easily be formed into an arrest/rescue formation. A wedge is a V-shaped formation with the point officer at the front and the remaining officers forming 45-degree angles on both flanks. Typically, the team leaders will center themselves within the wedge, and the squad leader will position himself near either the front or the rear of the formation.

Chemical Agents

Chemical agents are among the most common tools used by law enforcement for dispersing hostile crowds. There are a number of different reasons that officers may need to use chemical agents in the course of

FIGURE 3.4: *Chemical agents are commonly used when intervening in hostile crowds.*

their duties. Whether preventing an escape, dealing with a dangerous animal, or attempting to overcome the resistance of a noncompliant suspect, chemical agents offer a reasonably low-risk, less lethal alternative to other force tools available to police.

Chemical agents are particularly useful when dealing with large, hostile crowds and other civil disobedience situations. When properly used, they can be deployed with substantial standoff distance from any acts of violence, and can allow law enforcement officers to gain control over significant numbers of people at one time.

Once the agent is deployed and the crowd has dispersed, officers must focus on decontamination and cleanup of themselves, their equipment, and any citizens who might need their assistance.

It is important that police officers understand the terminology, capabilities, exposure symptoms, and decontamination procedures associated with commonly used chemical agents in order to be able to effectively handle and deploy them. It is also critical that officers understand how to use protective equipment, such as gas masks. Proper maintenance of equipment must also be learned so that the equipment works effectively in a location where chemical agents have been deployed.

Types of Chemical Agents

The three most common agents used in law enforcement are chloroacetophenone (CN), otho-chlorobenzylidene-molonitrile (CS), and oleoresin capsicum (OC). Commonly referred to by the generic term **tear gas**, the three agents are actually very different in their makeup, the way they affect people, and how they are deployed.

CN Agent

Chloroacetopenone (CN) was originally discovered by German scientists in the 1870s, but was not used to any extent until the 1920s, when the French military began to deploy it to break up riots in their colonies. By 1930, CN was being utilized by most developed nations' police agencies for the same purposes, and it is still used by many police agencies in the U.S. today.

CN is generally odorless, and is classified as a **lachrymator**, or tearing agent. It is five times heavier than air, and has the ability to displace oxygen in enclosed areas. Turning it into a fine vapor, which creates a blue-white cloud at the point of its release, best disperses it.

Because CN is deployed by use of a device that burns the chemical to create a fog, and because CN displaces oxygen, CN shouldn't be used inside structures where there is a potential for a fire hazard or in confined areas where people exposed to CN could also suffer asphyxia (suffocation).

Because of these limitations, CN has largely been replaced by ortho-chlorobenzylidene-molonitrile by most U.S. law enforcement agencies. Delivery devices that contain CN typically will have red color-code markings so that they can be recognized easily when stored with other chemical agents.

CS Agent

Ortho-chlorobenzylidene-molonitrile (CS) was originally discovered in 1928 by two American scientists, and later researched and developed by the British military in the 1950s. It has been widely used by U.S. law enforcement and the U.S. military since the 1960s. Some notable examples of its usage include the 1993 Waco siege by the FBI and the 2009 riots at the G-20 Summit in Pittsburgh, PA.

CS has a pungent pepper odor when burned, and is typically color-coded with blue markings. Like CN, CS is a lachrymator, and also has the ability to displace oxygen in enclosed areas. It is, however, much faster acting than CN and substantially less toxic. These factors have made CS a more attractive option for many law enforcement agencies when choosing a chemical agent for use in civil disobedience situations. It is most effective when deployed by burning, but can also be deployed through aerosol means. Like CN, CS is not optimum for use inside structures or in confined areas when deployed by use of a pyrotechnic device. However, it is often the best overall choice for use in an outdoor crowd control situation.

OC Agent

Oleoresin capsicum (OC) is often lumped in with CN and CS as a chemical agent because it is used in the same manner and in many of the same situations. However, oleoresin is a sticky, oily substance, and capsicum is the part of a pod-type pepper that makes it "hot" to the human taste. OC therefore is not a chemical at all, but is instead the sticky, oily, substance that is found in pod peppers.

Military units as far back as 1100 BC have used OC. Both India and China used crushed pepper "stink pots" to help move their enemies' forces around the battlefield and into defensive positions. However, it was not until 1973 that the FBI developed OC into a tool for modern law enforcement. Today, it is estimated that 97% of U.S. law enforcement officers carry OC as an individual intermediate weapon, while to most U.S. agencies keep OC crowd control devices in their inventories.

While similar to CN and CS in its intended use, OC is very different in the way that it affects the human body and how it is actually deployed. While CN and CS are considered lachrymators or irritants, OC is an inflammatory agent, meaning it causes a burning and swelling sensation on the body, particularly in the sinuses. In its liquid form, OC can come in a variety of colors, ranging from a light yellow-orange to a deep red.

Because OC is not a chemical, it is not a regulated substance like CN and CS. Most OC products are color coded with orange markings, but because of the lack of regulation, this is not an industry-wide practice. It is therefore important to read the label of any product believed to contain OC to ensure that this is, in fact, the case.

Exposure to OC affects the eyes, skin, nose, mouth, throat and lungs. The mucous membranes of the mouth, nose, and throat burn intensely and become swollen. The eyes also burn and typically twitch severely. If OC is inhaled into the lungs, exposed persons will cough violently, and may experience a gagging sensation and become short of breath.

Unlike CN and CS, OC cannot be deployed through the use of pyrotechnic devices, and is instead normally dispersed via aerosol. This makes OC a much safer option for use in confined spaces and in areas that may present fire hazards. As a result, OC continues to gain popularity every year with law enforcement agencies. However, because it is limited to dispersal by aerosol containers, OC is not always the best option for dealing with large crowds that span large open areas.

Methods for Deploying Chemical Agents

Modern technology allows police officers a variety of options with regard to chemical agents, not only in choosing which agent and which deployment type is most appropriate for each situation, but also in choosing which tool is best suited for deployment. There are four ways that chemical agents are commonly deployed: aerosol, fogging, pyrotechnics, and blast expulsion. There are also a variety of tools and devices that can be used by law enforcement to deploy chemical agents, ranging from small handheld canisters to hand-thrown grenades, grenade launchers, and large backpack and stationary fogging machines.

In law enforcement, the situation generally dictates which tactics, methods, and tools are most appropriate for accomplishing the given mission. The same is true when deploying chemical agents. In order for chemical agents to be safely and effectively used, considerations must be made for the following:

- Environmental conditions
- The proximity of people uninvolved the civil disobedience situation
- Fire hazards

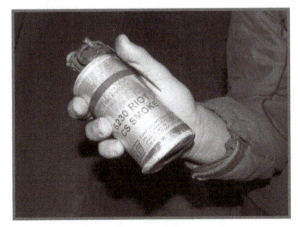

FIGURE 3.5: *Advances in technology have created various methods of delivery of chemical agents.*

As stated earlier, OC is most commonly deployed through the use of an aerosol device. Individual aerosol canisters ranging in size from two ounces to four ounces are the most common tool used by patrol officers and other police officers working in uniformed divisions. While suitable for subduing single perpetrators or small groups of people, small handheld units are generally not effective when dealing with crowds. Their range, dispersion area, and the total volume of agent they are able to put into the air are extremely limited. Hand-thrown **aerosol grenades**, which normally contain six ounces of agent or more, and larger one-pound and two-pound aerosol units that resemble small fire extinguishers, offer law enforcement officers a solution when they must be able to deploy the agent into confined places, near fire hazards, or when several officers need to be armed with small, portable devices that are easy to operate in simultaneously multiple locations.

CN is largely ineffective when deployed by aerosol, but in the 1980s aerosol-driven CS units became available. While not nearly as effective as CS when it is burned, or as OC in aerosol format, granulated CS can be deployed similarly to OC, and is available in aerosol grenades and in handheld aerosol units by a limited number of manufacturers.

The best way to deploy CS and CN is through heat. Fogging devices use hot gases to vaporize liquid CS and CN. The vaporized heated agent is then released into the air as a fog cloud. Deployment devices range in size from smaller, backpack-style units, to larger, vehicle-mounted fogging devices that can cover huge areas of open space if conditions are right.

When fire hazards are present, **foggers** can offer advantages over pyrotechnic devices. They have the ability to cover the large areas quickly, but are not suitable for use in confined spaces. They are also large, heavy, expensive, slow to deploy, and cannot be distributed between numerous officers or as easily moved to new locations as the smaller aerosol units.

The use of **pyrotechnic devices** is another way to apply heat to CS and CN for deployment. Common pyrotechnic devices include both hand-thrown grenades and grenades that are fired from 37mm and 40mm launchers. When a pyrotechnic device is deployed, a granulated form of the chemical agent is burned from within the grenade. The burning agent is released into the air as a cloud over a period of time while the fire continues to burn inside the grenade body. Pyrotechnic grenades are also commonly referred to as "continuous discharge" devices.

Pyrotechnic devices represent the highest fire hazard among chemical agent delivery methods. The actual fire inside the deploying device's body is a concern, but the extreme temperature that the body heats to is a concern as well. Pyrotechnic grenades have also been known to start structure fires in cases where they have accidentally been thrown or launched into loose debris or among flammable liquids.

While pyrotechnics represents the greatest fire risk among deployment methods, there are many crowd control situations where pyrotechnic deployment of CS or CN is the best possible solution. Burned CS and CN granules are more effective in incapacitating people than the heated liquid CS and CN commonly used in foggers. The capability to throw a grenade into an area deep within a crowd, over an obstruction, or around a corner without exposing the deploying officer to a potential threat, offers advantages as well.

Pyrotechnics fired from launchers have the ability to be deployed up to 200 yards away without requiring officers to get close to a hostile crowd. They can be deployed over even larger obstacles than hand-thrown devices. Additionally, many pyrotechnic devices are small, light, relatively inexpensive, and are very easy to operate and deploy. They can be moved around a crowd with little effort, as needed, and can be utilized by many officers at several locations simultaneously if necessary.

FIGURE 3.6: *Police officers have a number of tools at their disposal when dealing with crowd control.*

The tools and devices used to deploy chemical agents by blast expulsion are very similar to the tools and devices used to deploy chemical agents by pyrotechnic means. The way the agent leaves the device once it is deployed and enters the atmosphere is what is critically different.

Blast expulsion devices use explosive compounds to heat and deploy micropulverized chemical agents into the air. These devices are also referred to as instantaneous discharge or bursting devices. OC, CS, and CN can all be deployed through blast expulsion, but this method is not optimum for OC, because powdered OC is not nearly as effective at incapacitation as its liquid form. As a result, the vast majority of blast expulsion devices use CS and CN as their chemical agent.

Like pyrotechnics, the most common blast expulsion devices are hand-thrown grenades and grenades that are fired from 37mm and 40mm launchers. The two primary benefits of blast expulsion over pyrotechnics are that they are far less of a fire hazard than pyrotechnics, and through instantaneous discharge, immediately upon delivery, blast expulsion devices place chemical agents in a large area. Like foggers, however, the heated microparticles of CS or CN, while effective, are normally not as effective as their pyrotechnic counterparts.

Methods for Treating Chemical Agent Burns

Decontamination procedures for anyone exposed to chemical agents should begin as soon as the person has been properly restrained and officer safety is secured. Each agent discussed in this Module is different from the others, and each person exposed to agents is unique as well. As a result, the responses to exposure for agents are extremely varied. It is even possible that a person who is exposed to the same agent at two different times may have two completely different levels of reaction, depending on the conditions at the time of the exposure. How a person reacts and how quickly an officer can help that person through the recovery process can vary greatly, depending on the person's physical condition, psychological makeup, the degree of exposure to the agent, which agent the person was exposed to, and the influence of alcohol or drugs.

The single best treatment for exposure to any chemical agent is fresh air. If available, exposed and affected areas of the person's skin can be flushed with water and washed with a non-oily, tear-free soap such as baby shampoo. No salves, ointments, or moisturizing agents should be used on someone who has been exposed to crowd control chemical agents. Salves and ointments seal the chemical agent to the skin, don't allow air or water to wash away the agent, and cause continued discomfort. Commercially manufactured decontamination wipes are available in individually wrapped packages. These wipes are typically simple, cotton-based disposable cloths soaked in a water and tear-free soap solution that can be carried in the pocket or with other equipment. The wipes are convenient to use and can be made accessible to officers to initiate the decontamination process.

Whenever chemical agents are deployed in a location where a crowd is gathered or a riot is occurring, law enforcement officers should be prepared to establish a decontamination station for both officers and citizens who may become exposed. A contained area safely located away from the crowd, where air can flow freely and a fresh water source is available, is ideal. If available, fans that are designed for large area coverage are also recommended.

Officers should know basic procedures to administer self-decontamination and assist others with decontamination when affected by chemical agents. The primary areas that will require decontamination on any affected person are the eyes, skin, nose, and chest.

When eyes are exposed to chemical agents, the affected person should keep his eyes open and resist the natural tendency to allow them to seal shut. The affected person should face into the wind and keep his hands away from his eyes. Tearing helps to clear the eyes of agent particles and should be encouraged. Tears should be blotted away, and eyes should not be rubbed. If tearing and fresh air does not wash all of particles out of the eyes, large amounts of cool water applied to the eyes can provide significant relief while helping to flush the eyes.

Skin exposed to chemical agents will often experience a strong burning or stinging sensation, and blisters can form if the skin is exposed to the agent in heavy concentrations or for a prolonged period of time. To decontaminate the skin, exposed persons should sit still and attempt to reduce any sweating. Fresh air and the washing of any directly exposed skin with a mild soap and large amounts of water for a period of approximately 10 minutes is normally enough to decontaminate even the most grossly exposed person.

When chemical agents are inhaled through the nose, the most common symptoms are a strong burning sensation inside the nose and nasal discharge. A decontamination technique that is effective for exposed nasal passages is to blow the nose vigorously to remove any particles that have rested on the mucous membranes of the nose. If discomfort is severe, nose drops, or flushing the nose with fresh water, may help.

Chemical agents inhaled into the lungs can cause tightness in the chest that is often accompanied with a feeling of panic. Additionally, subjects who have inhaled agent particles into the lungs may experience severe coughing and a strong burning sensation in the chest. Time is the only thing that will decontaminate the lungs, though coughing will help to push out particles. Persons exposed should be encouraged to remain calm and to breathe normally. Reassuring someone who has inhaled particles will help to prevent panic as well.

CASE STUDY

Let's return to the protest group conducting a sit-in at the logging company headquarters. Several squads deployed in crowd control formations have been deployed, and orders for the crowd to disperse have been delivered. The crowd has refused to leave. The decision has been made to use force to move the crowd, and orders have been issued that any person who actively or passively resists being removed from the property will be arrested.

As your squad begins to move forward in a skirmish line, several members of the protest group become violent, and start picking up rocks, sticks, and other debris in the area. Each person in your squad is armed with a riot baton, and is issued a riot shield, a gas mask, and a helmet for defense. Additionally, each team leader has been issued a one-pound OC aerosol handheld unit, and your squad leader has been issued a 37mm launcher and three launchable CS pyrotechnic grenades.

The crowd is outdoors, within a large fenced-in parking area with only routes allowing personnel in or out. Formations are moving in a manner to attempt to channel all of the protestors toward one exit route, but the protestors are not budging. All the company's managers and employees have either left the area or have returned to the building and are observing the situation through their windows. The media is still on the scene, and several news cameras are recording events. As the distance between officers and protestors gets within 20 yards, the protestors begin throwing their rocks and debris.

What is the best response to this situation, given the information provided?

Can chemical agents be deployed safely in this situation? If so, what are some of the ways to utilize the chemical agents you have available? What factors must be considered regarding the use of chemical agents in the described situation? What circumstances might cause the squad leader or other law enforcement supervisors to decide not to deploy the chemical agents they have available?

Assuming that you decide that the best course of action is to utilize your chemical weapons to help ensure officer and public safety and quickly restore order, what are the next steps that need to be taken after arrests have been made, the crowd has been dispersed, and all officers in your squad have been accounted for?

Summary

Crowd control and civil disobedience situations are unique, fluid, evolving, and at times volatile situations. Law enforcement officers are expected to protect the right of citizens to freely and peacefully assemble, while keeping other citizens and their property safe.

In the event that unlawful acts unfold at a public gathering, there are several tactics and tools available to help law enforcement restore order. Law enforcement officers are expected to understand these tactics and have access to the proper tools for crowd control situations. They must utilize training and experience and base their decisions on the totality of the circumstances known at the time.

Specialized formations of officers that are quickly deployed are fundamental to the initial response. Based on the situation, a variety of chemical agents, including tear gas, are used to disperse crowds. Officers need to know the types of agents available and when it is appropriate to use them. If chemical agents are deployed, first aid response for the affected parties is essential. All officers must know how to identify and treat those who have adverse reactions.

Discussion Questions

1. What might occur within a crowd of people that would change a legal protest into a situation where the rights of others have been violated and law enforcement must respond?

2. How does the terrain affect which crowd control formation a squad leader chooses when responding to a riot situation?

3. Why would a wedge formation be preferred over a skirmish line when trying to move a crowd from around a corner of a building or into an alley or side street?

4. Discuss the role of chemical agents in a crowd control situation. When would they be appropriate for use? Under what circumstances would they not be appropriate?

5. Discuss the differences in CN, CS, and OC. How do they differ in use? Why would a squad leader choose one agent over another in different crowd control situations?

6. Discuss the different methods for deploying chemical agents. When would use of a launching device be preferred over hand-thrown grenades or foggers? What hazards or drawbacks could be associated with using a launcher?

Key Terms

Aerosol grenades — Devices formulated to release their contents in a vapor cloud. They are typically hand thrown and require no fuse or explosive charge to disseminate their contents.

Blast expulsions — Devices designed to release their contents through use of an explosive blast. They may be fired from a launcher or be hand thrown.

Chemical agent — A generic term used to describe all irritant and inflammatory agents used by law enforcement for crowd control.

Chloroacetophenone — The scientific name for the irritant chemical agent commonly known as CN.

Column formation — A crowd control formation that is normally used to move a squad from one location to another, to divide a crowd, or as a lead-in to other formations.

Civil disobedience — Refusal to obey governmental demands or commands as a collective means of forcing concessions from the government.

Crowd control formation — The tactical grouping of squads of law enforcement officers for crowd control purposes.

Diagonal formation — Also referred to as an echelon formation, the diagonal formation uses a slanted line of officers to clear crowds from the side of a building or wall, or to change the direction of a crowd.

Dispersal order — An order given at the scene of a crowd control situation that states that an event has been declared unlawful and that all persons in the area must disperse.

Foggers — Devices used to disperse large amounts of chemical agents with short- to medium-range capability.

Free assembly — The individual right to come together and collectively express, promote, pursue, or defend common interests. This right is protected by the First Ammendment of the U.S. Constitution.

Lachrymator — A tear-producing substance.

Oleoresin capsicum — The oily, sticky, substance found in peppers that acts as an inflammatory.

Otho-chlorobenzylidene-molonitrile — The scientific name for the irritant chemical agent commonly known as CS.

Point officer — The officer placed at the front and center in most crowd control formations who typically has first contact with the crowd.

Pyrotechnics — The art of making or manufacturing of, and the use of, fire-producing devices.

Rescue formation — A crowd control formation that is used to affect arrests or rescue people located inside a hostile or potentially hostile crowd.

Riot — A tumultuous disturbance of the public peace by three or more persons assembled together and acting with a common intent.

Skirmish line — A crowd control formation that is used to move small crowds in a specific direction, to block access to restricted areas, or to contain a group within a specific area.

Squad leader — Direct report to a platoon leader or the tactical commander in a crowd control situation. They give all orders related to assembly, formation, and movement of the squad, and assign the remaining members of the formation as the point officer, team leaders, or squad members.

Team leader — Direct report to a squad leader in a crowd control formation. They are typically more senior officers within the squad, and often-placed in charge of any special weapons or tools assigned to the squad, such as chemical agents or less lethal weapons systems.

Tear gas — A gaseous substance, which upon dispersal in the atmosphere irritates mucus membranes. It is used chiefly in dispelling mobs.

Wedge formation — A crowd control formation that is used to break a crowd into smaller sections or to penetrate a crowd for short distances.

MODULE 4

Bombs and Explosive Devices

Key Module Concepts:

- The major categories of improvised explosive devices (IED)

- Common military munitions

- Recommended procedures for dealing with bomb threats

- Bomb search techniques

- Activities for the dispatch phase of the post-blast response

Introduction

The fear of terrorism that developed as a result of the September 11, 2001 attacks is unsettling. Images of improvised explosive device attacks on United States military personnel continue to be reported via media sources and the Internet, and stories about shoe bombers intending to take down aircrafts and high volumes of explosive materials illegally crossing into the United States from the southern border have become a fairly common occurrence over the past decade. Of great concern is the fact that explosives are the weapons of choice for terrorist organizations around the world.

As a general rule, since 2001 law enforcement agencies in the U.S. have significantly increased their budgets related to training and their capacity to deal with explosive threats. In addition, many valuable lessons have been learned, and best practices related to blast site investigations, improvised explosive devices, and terrorist employment of explosives have been modeled from military and federal law enforcement activities in the war zones of Iraq and Afghanistan.

Law enforcement agencies in the U.S. have always required their officers to have some measure of training and familiarity with explosives. Commercial, military, and homemade explosive devices may be found at crime scenes, on abandoned properties, and even in public parks and recreational areas throughout the country. However, the rise of both domestic and international terrorism, and the increase in the use of explosives as a means of attack, has created a need for officers to receive further training in, and increased awareness of, what explosives are, what they can do, and the hazards associated with their deployment. This Module provides a basic introduction to bombs and explosive devices, and common procedures to follow when dealing with these weapons.

Explosive devices and bombs have become an increasingly popular form of attack for criminals and terrorists. What are some motivating factors for a perpetrator to choose a bomb over another weapon or tool to commit a crime or perform a terrorist act?

Ask Yourself

- *How difficult is it to create a bomb? Where would a criminal or a terrorist obtain the components required to construct an explosive device?*

- *What purpose do bomb threats serve? Why wouldn't a perpetrator simply detonate a device, rather than notify an intended victim in advance?*

- *Does a bomb actually have to detonate to be successful?*

FIGURE 4.1: *The Alfred P. Murrah Building, post-Oklahoma City Bombing*

Device Recognition

There is no one standard related to what a bomb is supposed to look like. Bombs can be built with common household materials as their primary components, professionally constructed with commercial explosive materials, or built with military **munitions** (or military-grade ammunition). Bombs can be concealed in something as small and as simple as a paper envelope, or weigh several tons that must be moved around by large trucks. Amateur bombers may utilize relatively obvious construction techniques to craft simple devices such as pipe bombs. Professional criminals and terrorists, on the other hand, have the capability to create intricate devices that are easily concealed or camouflaged to look like something completely different than what they actually are.

Recognizing an explosive device is rarely easy. Bombers typically do not want their devices to be found, and will normally take great measures to make sure they are not. When attempting to locate an explosive device, whether responding to a **bomb threat** call, executing a search warrant where bombs may be involved, or conducting a tactical entry where explosives have knowingly been placed (such as the Columbine High School massacre in Littleton, Colorado in 1999), the key is not to look for overt devices, but instead to pay attention and look for objects that are out of place or simply do not look like they belong in the immediate environment.

Did You Know?

Letter and parcel bombs are among the most common explosive devices used by criminals in the U.S. Much information is available through a variety of public sources regarding recognition of these types of devices. Some common factors that would cause a letter or parcel to be suspicious would include oil stains on the exterior of the parcel, no return address label, a letter that feels rigid, uneven, or lopsided, and the excessive use of postage.

Bombs and explosive devices are threats that neither law enforcement officers nor civilians should take lightly. Bombs have the capability to cause mass casualties and damage significant amounts of property. Even the threat of a bomb has the ability to create hysteria and chaos among the general public. Officers who deal with explosive devices should receive extensive training specific to their detection, handling, care and disposal.

Unless a law enforcement officer is assigned to a bomb disposal unit and has received the requisite training, any object suspected of containing an explosive device should be left alone. Officers who are not trained in bomb disposal should establish a perimeter, conduct an evacuation of the area, and maintain order until qualified bomb technicians arrive on the scene.

FIGURE 4.2: *An IED made with a 200-grain detonation cord, disguised as an electrical extension cord.*

Improvised Explosive Devices

An **improvised explosive device (IED)** can be made to look like almost anything, and can use a wide variety of commercial, military, or locally produced explosive materials and initiators. An IED is a "homemade" device that is designed to cause death or injury by using explosives alone or in combination with **shrapnel** (materials that are produced from a bomb, shell, or mine fragments), chemicals, biological toxins, or radiological material. IEDs can be produced in various sizes, functioning methods, containers, and delivery methods. They can be concealed in just about any container, and can be triggered by almost any means. They range from simple pipe bombs with cannon fuses, to letter and package bombs, to highly advanced shaped charge devices that fire armor-penetrating plates and are initiated by infrared triggers.

IEDs are unique in nature because the bomb maker must improvise with whatever materials are available. Designed to defeat a specific target or type of target, they generally become more difficult to detect and protect against as they become more sophisticated. They are a popular choice for attacks among criminals and terrorists because they typically leave very little evidence for investigators, maintain the anonymity of the bomber, and create escalated fear and confusion. Additionally, the devices don't have to necessarily detonate to achieve the goal of causing terror.

Although they can vary widely in shape and form, IEDs share a common set of components that include an initiation system or fuse, an explosive compound, a detonator, and a container that is normally used for concealment purposes. All IEDs are characterized by varying detonation techniques and fall into four major categories: time delayed, victim activated booby traps, environmental (activated by a thermostat, humidity, etc.) and command detonated IEDs. They may be subcategorized in a number of additional ways.

IEDs are similar to mines in that they are usually designed to kill or incapacitate personnel or destroy vehicles. They are also placed to avoid detection and improve their effectiveness. Most are victim-activated, but some may involve remote or command detonation architectures. When well designed, IEDs can be highly effective and can be used to attack just about any target imaginable, ranging from individuals and vehicles to aircraft and buildings.

The use of IEDs is limited only by the imagination of the criminal or terrorist employing it. It is important to understand that when dealing with IEDs, there is no such thing as a stereotypical device.

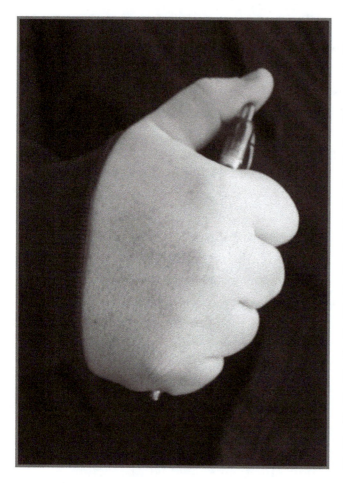

FIGURE 4.3: *A small blasting cap IED disguised in a common ballpoint pen.*

Munitions

Although in recent years there has been a demonstrated innovation in the fabrication of improvised explosive devices, conventional military weapons and munitions have been used in numerous criminal and terrorist attacks as well. These weapons range from highly sophisticated shoulder-fired air defense missiles to traditional grenades, rocket propelled grenades and mines.

Explosives

There are a variety of explosive compounds that are used in military munitions. They come in liquid, gas, and solid form, and are then formed into several different types of blocks, cords, granules, and flakes. They can be used by themselves or can be combined with other explosive compounds to create a more effective blast.

All explosive ordnance and munitions require an explosive compound to detonate. Common explosive compounds include **dynamite**, C4, and **trinitrotoluene** (TNT).

- Dynamite comes in all shapes and sizes, but is most commonly produced as a 6-8 inch long cylinder that is 1-3 inches in diameter. It has an expansion rate of 22,000 feet per second.

- C4 and other "plastic" explosives are widely sought out by terrorist organizations, as they are easily shaped and extremely stable

- TNT is one of the most common military and industrial explosives due to its stable nature, insensitivity to shock and friction, and its high expansion rate. A common misconception is that dynamite and TNT are the same thing, or that TNT is a component of dynamite. TNT is a specific explosive compound typically found in flake form, and dynamite is an absorbent compound soaked in nitroglycerin that is compressed and formed into cylinders.

Grenades

Grenades are used by both domestic and international terrorists and militia organizations. In their 1998 annual report on terrorist activities, HAMAS stated that a combination of time-delayed bombs coupled with commando attacks using hand grenades comprised the major part of effective operations in an attack and caused the most casualties. This publication is easily found on the Internet, and has been taken as evidence at numerous crime scenes in the U.S. related to domestic and international terrorism.

Small and relatively easy to conceal, both U.S. military fragmentation grenades and foreign military grenades are confiscated regularly by law enforcement officers around the United States. Many grenades are stolen from military bases by current and former military personnel; some have been brought, undetected, into the country as war trophies. Typically simple in design, most fragmentation grenades are time-delayed explosive devices that consist of a cast iron body, an explosive charge, and a detonator. Their weight and dimensions can vary, but most modern fragmentation grenades weigh approximately one pound, and are approximately four inches in length. The average person can throw a fragmentation grenade 30 to 35 meters. Most modern fragmentation grenades have a casualty radius of approximately 15 meters, and a fatality radius of 5 meters, but can disperse fragments up to 250 meters.

Rocket Propelled Grenades

A rocket propelled grenade (RPG) system fires a motorized grenade from a tube-like launcher. Although it is an unguided weapon, a trained operator can engage targets at surprisingly long distances. The RPG is a favored weapon system for many international terrorist organizations, and has been used against law enforcement and military targets all over the world. Originally developed as an anti-tank weapon system, they have also been used as anti-aircraft weapons and are highly effective against personnel and buildings. RPGs are relatively simple devices. Many armies use RPG systems extensively, which means that a great number of people are trained and experienced in their use. They are also widely available on the international weapons black market.

Bombs and Artillery

Although most bombs used by terrorists are improvised or fabricated devices, conventional munitions have been used on occasion, especially in the form of booby traps. Bombs, artillery shells, and mortar rounds have all been recovered at crime scenes and by search warrants throughout the U.S. Additionally, several times a year, local, state, and federal law enforcement agencies are called to recover aged munitions that are found in national parks, residential subdivisions, and rural properties that were built over old military training facilities and bombing ranges. The occasions where law enforcement officers come into contact with substantial military ordnance are much more common than most people would think.

CASE STUDY

IEDs have become increasingly complex over the past several years and have become more and more popular among both domestic and international terrorists as tools for causing injury, death, and destruction of property. Just as law enforcement personnel have learned valuable lessons on how to react, counter, and even defuse IEDs from the military and law enforcement operations in Iraq and Afghanistan, international terrorist organizations and criminal elements are also learning from those engagements, sharing information, and becoming better at their craft.

India's National Security Guard (NSG) is a federal government special response unit that is tasked with counter-terrorism activities. The NSG Training Center is an internationally acclaimed Center of Excellence, and the NSG National Bomb Data Center is known for hosting some of the most progressive and advanced law enforcement explosives training programs in Asia. As a result, NSG bomb technicians are among the best in the world.

As evidenced in the September 2008 bomb incident in Delhi, India, bombs are now appearing all over the globe that even the best bomb technicians utilizing the best equipment available are unable to defuse. During this event, NSG technicians located explosive devices at India Gate and in Central Park that could not be rendered safe despite their best efforts. Ultimately, the bombs were loaded into highly sophisticated bomb disposal equipment known as a Total Containment Vessel (TCV and intentionally detonated with no harm to any personnel, equipment, or buildings in the immediate area.

TCVs are relatively common in the U.S. among law enforcement agencies in major metropolitan areas that maintain dedicated bomb squads. They are, however, cost prohibitive for most small and mid-sized agencies. With the number of bomb incidents in the U.S. climbing, and the complexity of bombs growing continuously, it is important that law enforcement managers and administrators at agencies that do not have access to dedicated bomb squads or advanced equipment begin to look at creative solutions to resolve these complicated problems.

Mines

Mines are also used by terrorist organizations to inflict damage. Classified as either anti-personnel or anti-tank, mines are traditionally used by military forces to deny an enemy access to an area or to channel their movements. Terrorists and other criminals have used mines on a global scale, but unlike conventional military forces, terrorists use mines to disrupt social, economic, and political operations. Consequently, mines are often placed around schools, on walking paths, and in crowded areas in order to gain terror effects.

There are literally hundreds of different types of mines. They come in many shapes and sizes, are made of materials varying from wood to plastic to steel, and can be detonated in a variety of different ways, including the use of pressure switches, command detonation, and time detonation. "Smart" mines are the latest technological advancement in mines; these can distinguish between potential targets. Mines are manufactured by almost every developed nation's military establishment and are a common product on the international arms black market. The most common mines used by criminals and terrorists include models that originate from many of the former Warsaw Pact countries, the United States, China, Britain and Iran.

Response Plans

Actual bombings in the U.S. are relatively rare. Bomb threats, however, are fairly common. While it is under-stood that most bomb threats are false, the amount of injury and destruction a bomb can cause warrants that all threats be investigated, and often searches must be conducted in order to confirm the absence of a real threat.

FIGURE 4.5: *Thoughtful and well-executed responses to bomb threats are essential to public safety.*

Developing a response plan for bomb threats and potential incidents is the responsibility of individual business owners and managers. While law enforcement will be required to conduct an investigation of any threats made, their actions will not begin until well after the perpetrator has delivered his threat, dispatch has been notified, and officers have been sent to the scene. Plans made and actions taken by company management prior to the arrival of officers will greatly influence law enforcement's ability be successful in its investigation, and will also dictate how searches will be conducted.

Law enforcement can offer advice, fundamental education and training to local businesses on the proper way to handle bomb threats and conduct bomb searches, and can assist in the process of conducting actual searches if requested. Providing these services will foster improved community relations, help to maintain community safety and security, and should be encouraged. As a result, law enforcement officers need to be well versed in common bomb search techniques and be educated on the proper way to handle bomb threats when they are made so that they can provide assistance to the community when needed.

Bomb Threats

Bomb threats are messages, usually delivered in verbal or written form, that state an intent to detonate an explosive, or **incendiary**, device to cause property damage, death, or injuries. Most commonly delivered by telephone, the vast majority of bomb threats made in the U.S. are intended to cause disruption, or delivered as practical jokes, rather than an actual warning of real devices. The Bureau of Alcohol Tobacco and Firearms estimates that less than 1% of bomb threats made in the U.S. are real.

Criminal statutes in all 50 states dictate severe penalties for making bomb threats, whether there is a real device planted or not. For example, in Massachusetts, making a bomb threat is a felony offense and if convicted, the person making the threat could face up to 20 years in prison, up to a $50,000 fine, and be made to pay restitution for the costs of the disruption. In New York, bomb threats are classified as "E" felonies. Additionally, making a false bomb threat is a federal offense, punishable under U.S. Code 18-844e with a penalty of up to 10 years in prison, a $250,000 fine, or both.

Did You Know?

U.S. Code 18-844e, Part 1, Chapter 40 is the U.S. federal law that establishes crimes and criminal procedures for the illegal importation, manufacture, distribution, and storage of explosive materials.

Bomb threats that are not pranks are often made to support other criminal acts, such as extortion, arson, or robbery and are used as diversions or as tools to scare the intended victim into a desired behavior pattern. Actual bombings that are terrorist actions or intended to destroy property or commit murder are typically perpetrated without any prior warning.

There are three basic courses of action that can be taken in response to a bomb threat. The threat can be ignored, a decision can be made to evacuate the area or facility that is being threatened, or a search can be initiated with a follow-up evacuation planned, if warranted. Law enforcement officers dispatched to a bomb threat scene must understand that the decision to evacuate an area or building rests on the threatened party. Unless there is evidence that the threat of property damage or human life being taken can be substantiated as real, officers' duties are to assist, advise and investigate. Responding officers may be called upon to assist in an evacuation or the search of a threatened area, but do not have the authority to make a business or an individual do anything until the presence of an actual device is confirmed.

Ignoring a bomb threat is never the correct response, but immediate evacuation upon the receipt of a bomb threat can cause a severe disruption in business, costing the victim substantial amounts of money in lost productivity. In fact, this is often the intended purpose of the perpetrator's call. Bomb threats are also made by professional criminals and terrorists in advance of planting real explosive devices as a means of gathering information and intelligence related to evacuation routes, evacuation times, the number of people on site at a given time, and so on.

Typically, initiating a **bomb search** is the best overall course of action, with a plan to evacuate the area in the event that a device is actually found. Threatened companies may choose to perform a search with their own personnel, or may request that law enforcement officers assist them, or conduct the search for them. How a search is organized and conducted is the decision of the threatened business or individual, but businesses not accustomed to receiving threats will not have detailed search plans or adequately trained personnel on site, and will request that local law enforcement become involved in this process.

Did You Know?

The most serious of all decisions to be made by a company's management team in the event of a bomb threat is whether to evacuate the building. In many cases, this decision may have already been made during the development of the bomb incident plan. Making the decision whether or not to evacuate a building in the event of a bomb threat must balance the benefits of providing a safe environment for personnel in the building with the willingness to accept the physical and financial costs associated with the loss of labor time.

Procedures

From a procedural standpoint, it is important for potential victims to determine who within their organization would be most likely to receive a bomb threat. Once identified, training should be provided to those people to help them respond to the caller with appropriate questions, detail the conversation with the caller accurately, and report the threat to the appropriate authorities. In the event that law enforcement is called to the scene of a threat, having properly trained on-site personnel involved from the onset will be of great assistance. Whenever possible, law enforcement agencies should offer training to businesses and individuals that may be targets for bomb threats and establish specific protocol and procedures that will be adhered to in the event of a threat. This procedure will help to build a better relationship with the community, aid officers in conducting successful investigations in the event of a threat, and help to reduce panic or fear among citizens if or when a threat is actually made.

Bomb Searches

Most communities lack the ability to supply the number of law enforcement officers it would take to make a fast and thorough search of a facility of any size, and would be hard pressed to even fully staff a proper search of even a mid-sized search at a location such as a warehouse or a large department store. Even if such manpower were available, police officers are often not the most qualified people to conduct a search. Understanding that a criminal will not label his device with the word "bomb," and will most likely attempt to conceal his weapon in some way, the team undertaking a bomb search must have guidelines to help them identify an explosive device.

It is a fundamental rule that the best search is conducted by persons who are familiar with the area, in order to notice any strange or foreign object that is new to the environment or that has recently changed. However, the use of on-site personnel in the search may present problems with the hysteria that can result from the threat. Careful planning prior to an event can prevent this reaction. Businesses that have become the victims of a bomb threat can also ask law enforcement to intervene and take over the search, or at a minimum assist their personnel in conducting the search.

Frequently, companies that incur a high number of bomb threats do not want their staff alerted to the potential problem, and will utilize codes in order to notify key staff members that have been trained in conducting searches to respond and begin a search. For example, if the facility has a public address system, key personnel might be alerted to commence the search by use of a code signal, for example, "Mr. Oppenheimer, please come to the office." In these situations, law enforcement officers will rarely be utilized to assist in the search, because their presence would alert non-searching members of the company's staff of a potential problem, resulting in unwanted chaos.

A search plan for the building or premises should be developed before beginning the actual search, in order to assist law enforcement that may become involved. A basic search plan should divide the building to be searched into zones, with each person on the search team assigned a room or area within those zones. Personnel so assigned should make a survey of the area and note what objects normally occupy the area prior to conducting their actual search.

Searches conducted by management or law enforcement agents that are not personally familiar with the workspace are estimated to be 50-65% thorough. Typically, these searches are superficial, and are conducted in a way so that the general staff are never advised of the threat. Searches by employees who are intimately familiar with the immediate area are estimated to be 80-90% thorough; however, those searches require training of a larger group of people and can only be conducted in an overt manner. Team searches, where two or more people conduct an area search, are estimated to be 90-100% effective and are the preferred method under most circumstances.

Personnel conducting the search should be advised that in the event that they find something suspicious, they are not to touch or disturb the object in any way. Whenever possible, teams of two or more people should search each designated area. When a suspect device is found by one person, confirmation of suspicion should be provided by the second member of the team. In the event that it is not feasible to work in pairs, when a suspicious object is found, another solo searcher should be dispatched to the location of the object to confirm that it is out of the ordinary before taking any further action.

In some instances, the detonation or ignition of any explosive or incendiary device might depend on a change in environment, such as temperature variations or the presence of an electric current. Therefore, the personnel assigned to conduct a search should be cautioned not to cause any change in the environment; if that is not possible, they should alter the environment as minimally as possible.

Schools As Targets

Schools are among the most commonly targeted locations for both bomb threats and actual explosive attacks. The FBI reports that roughly 5% of all bomb incidents in the U.S. target schools. Between 1990 and 2002, the Bureau of Alcohol Tobacco and Firearms recorded 1,055 bomb incidents on school properties. Of those 1,055 bomb incidents, only 14 were accompanied by a warning to the school or other authorities. National statistics on bomb threats do not exist, but the number of bomb threats that many school districts across America receive is alarming. For example, during the 1997-1998 academic year, a Maryland school district reported a total of 150 bomb threats and 55 associated arrests.

While schools in the U.S. and abroad have been attacked and threatened by adult offenders, more often than not, juveniles are the offenders. Juveniles are responsible for an average of 35% of all actual bombing incidents at any location throughout the U.S. each year. In some states, juveniles have been responsible for up to 66% of all bombings.

Motivations for children to attack schools are vast and include the following underlying reasons:

- Humor
- Self assertion
- Anger
- Manipulation
- Aggression
- Hate and devaluation, omnipotence, fantasy, psychotic distortion, ideology, and retaliation

However, the research on motives is generally limited to other kinds of violence, rather than bomb threats and attacks, so any assessment of the motives of those who deliver bomb threats or actually place explosive devices remains speculative.

Did You Know?

The occurrence of bomb incidents and bomb threats at schools can have substantial impact on their victims, depending on how a school responds. The potential for serious injury and damage makes even an empty threat a very serious incident. The evacuation of buildings causes disruption to normal school activity, which, in many cases, may be the desired outcome from the attacker's point of view.

Many school districts report substantial financial losses because of school closings and costs of bomb search squads. School districts are also increasingly requiring schools to make up days lost due to bomb threats.

Unfortunately, school bombings and bomb threats are not a recent trend. The first recorded school bombing in the U.S. occurred in May of 1927 in Bath, Michigan, when a local farmer blew up a local schoolhouse killing 38 pupils, six adults, and injuring another 40 pupils. Equally unfortunate is that school-related explosive incidents occur at an alarming rate each year, and no decrease in occurrences is expected any time in the near future. After the Columbine High School incident of 1999, where a school massacre involving firearms and multiple improvised explosive devices were utilized, a national poll showed that 70% of respondents believed that the same thing could easily happen in their community. As a result, bomb threats directed at schools must be taken seriously and thoroughly investigated on every occurrence. Law enforcement officials should do everything in their power to safeguard their community's schools against such attacks.

Post-Blast Procedure

Post-blast response to a bomb scene takes place after an explosion has occurred. An explosives event has the potential to overwhelm first responders because of the large number of injuries, fatalities, and the extensive property destruction in the immediate area. It is important that law enforcement officers be trained to safely respond to these incidents.

It is impossible to plan for every type of explosives attack situation. However, the probability of law enforcement agencies encountering IEDs during their day-to-day activities is growing. As terrorism continues to be an ongoing and increasing domestic threat, law enforcement officers must commit themselves to continued education and training in post-blast incident response.

All public agencies responding to a blast scene share some of the same priorities during an explosives event, including life safety and incident stabilization. Planning and interagency cooperation for any terrorist or criminal attack type of event are paramount. Planning for blast incidents should be conducted long before an attack becomes a reality. Training should be coordinated among all agencies that may become involved in a blast response so that in the event of an attack, each responding agency already understands its roles and responsibilities upon arrival at the scene. Post-blast response activities should be broken down into steps that provide guidelines for responders at each phase of the event. Phases that are planned should include an initial dispatch and response phase, actions upon arrival at the scene, and post-blast response operations. After the scene is secured and order is restored, considerations must be made regarding crime scene maintenance and processing.

Dispatch and Response Phase

When an initial call is made regarding a blast incident, it is critical that all information available is provided to all responding units, and that the information provided is consistent among agencies. The nature of the call and the exact location are vitally important. In the past, agencies have advised responding officers to discontinue the use of cell phones and radios as they approach blast incident locations or areas where bomb threats have been made. It was feared that electronic signals emitted from these devices could trigger the bomb or any **secondary devices**, which are designed to activate after the primary device in order to kill or injure first responders, in the vicinity.

Today, it is generally accepted that the use of cell phones and radios are required in order to provide a rapid, coordinated response. While responders may be required to discontinue their use of cell phone and radios once they get within a very close distance of the blast site, or **hot zone**, these devices will continued to be utilized until the last possible moment, at which point other resources such as runners or hand and arm signals may be used for communication purposes within the immediate area.

Actions on Arrival

Units and personnel from multiple law enforcement, EMS, and fire agencies are likely to respond to the scene of any major blast incident. Establishing solid command and control of the scene and maintaining accountability of all personnel and equipment will be crucial to successful management of the scene.

One of the first responsibilities law enforcement officers will need to assume is the immediate dispersal of any crowds and the establishment of an outer perimeter, or a boundary to protect the crime scene. A staging area, which limits and accounts for the actions of all responders, should also be established.

When approaching the aftermath of a blast, proceed with extreme caution. Criminals and terrorists alike have been known to detonate explosive devices, wait for first responders to arrive on the scene, and then detonate secondary devices that specifically target those responders. Additionally, there may be a number of different secondhand hazards, ranging from downed electrical wires to loose falling debris in the area.

When possible, officers should approach a blast scene from uphill and upwind, then slow down and conduct a 360° scan of the scene before moving into the immediate area. Officers should be advised to look for objects and people that seem out of place. If something looks suspicious, it probably is.

Law enforcement officers should avoid entering actual blast areas, or hot zones, unless it is both necessary and possible to save lives. Firefighters and EMS personnel will be better trained and equipped to deal with activity in the hot zone. Only trained bomb technicians and explosive canine teams should be involved in any searches for secondary explosive devices. Other law enforcement personnel should focus on assisting in the establishment of hazard control zones around the incident (hot, warm, and cold), as well as staffing lookout or observer posts to watch the scene for additional threats.

FIGURE 4.6: *The aftermath of the bombing attack on the U.S. Embassy at Kenya.*

Post-Blast Response Operations

An explosion may result in a large number of victims with traumatic injuries. After a perimeter is secured, hazard zones have been established, and observer posts have been manned, law enforcement officers may be asked to assist in searching for victims or in the processing of the crime scene.

It may be necessary to search beyond the immediate blast scene for victims who are not able to call for help, such as the elderly who may be suffering from a health condition. In a dense urban environment, persons in upper stories of buildings may be injured or affected by the attack. Law enforcement officers who are not members of a bomb squad or a canine explosive detection team may be better suited for conducting these types of searches in the warm and cold zones, so that those with more training in explosive detection and blast response can focus their attention on the hot zone. Note that some seriously injured victims may have no visible wounds at all, and that some victims may be beyond help. Officers should expect to see a variety of traumatic injuries, including blast pressure or internal injuries, burns, and shrapnel wounds.

During a search of a warm or cold zone, officers should be aware of secondary hazards, such as unstable structures, damaged utilities, hanging debris, void spaces, falling pieces of broken glass, and other physical hazards. While a structure or object may not appear to have been affected on the surface from a blast, pressure waves caused by a major blast can travel great distances and deliver substantial amounts of force well outside the hot zone that can weaken structures and cause hazards. Officers should also continue to be aware of the possibility of secondary devices and attacks until the entire area has been cleared by bomb technicians and canine units.

Considerations

Blast sites can be extremely difficult to manage, due to the complexity of dealing with multiple responding agencies, the potential size of the perimeter required, the media attention they draw, and the hysteria created within the general public.

As a rule of thumb, the crime scene perimeter should extend 50% farther than the distance from the center of the initial blast to the location of the farthest piece of evidence found. Numerous non-law enforcement personnel will have to have access to the crime scene perimeter during the early phases of blast response in order to eliminate fires, rescue and provide medical treatment to victims, and to search for both persons killed by the blast and for secondary devices. Law enforcement should ensure that all responders take any and all measures necessary to preserve possible evidence for subsequent criminal and forensic investigations. Firefighters, for example, should not be allowed to conduct overhaul and clean-up operations until law enforcement investigators have authorized such activities.

An intensive media response should be expected. Senior law enforcement managers should appoint a public information officer to interact with the media, and all media questions should be routed through this person. Police officers working the blast scene should not provide interviews or any other information to anyone outside of their chain of command without prior approval. Friends and family of victims, as well as curious members of the general public, will most likely converge on the scene quickly. Family Assistance Centers should be established quickly after the crime scene perimeter is established in order to provide support to family members and keep distractions at the crime scene to a minimum.

Law enforcement officers assigned to a blast site crime scene should plan on an extensive, multi-day crime scene investigation. Lighting of the crime scene will most likely need to be planned so that processing can continue into night hours. Hazards associated with building damage after a blast often require that utilities be turned off, and it is probable that lights that are organic to the building will be damaged or inoperable.

The single most important rule to follow if assigned to a blast site crime scene is not to attempt to approach, move, handle, or disarm any confirmed or suspected device that is located. That is a job that is reserved for trained personnel.

Summary

Over the past few decades, the use of bombs and explosive devices by criminals and terrorist organizations against both persons and property has increased. Whether discussing a group of teens experimenting with pipe bombs in an abandoned warehouse district, or domestic and international terrorist attacks like those conducted by Timothy McVeigh in Oklahoma City or Al Qaeda in New York City in 1993, the mere mention of bombs or bombings creates a feeling of tension and fear among most Americans. As a result, law enforcement agencies have introduced specialized explosive and bomb scene training, equipment and countermeasures to their personnel.

When dealing with bombs and explosive devices, officer and public safety concerns are paramount. Any situation where a bomb is even potentially involved has the ability to cause chaos and hysteria. Depending on the size of the explosion, blast sites can quickly become extremely complex crime scenes that are incredibly difficult to manage. In order to keep themselves and the public they are charged to protect safe, law enforcement officers must familiarize themselves with bombs and explosive devices and the common procedures that are used to manage bomb investigations and crime scenes.

Discussion Questions

1. What type of questions might the call-taker or dispatcher ask a perpetrator who is calling in a bomb threat? What information is important to obtain?

2. Where would a criminal or a terrorist gain information or learn how to construct an IED? What are some ways that the terrorist would go about obtaining the materials needed to construct an explosive device?

3. Discuss the role of a patrol officer in the management of an explosive blast crime scene.

4. Discuss military munitions and how they might be obtained and utilized in criminal or terrorist acts. Who within the general public would have training and experience handling munitions or be capable of utilizing munitions to perpetrate a crime?

5. When responding to a call for service related to a bomb threat, what is the role of law enforcement? Why are officers not able to make decisions regarding the evacuation of buildings or conducting searches unless requested to do so by a threatened company's management team?

Key Terms

Bomb search — A physical search conducted by individuals or teams to locate explosive or incendiary devices.

Bomb threat — A verbal or written threat threatening to detonate an explosive or incendiary device to cause property damage or injuries.

Detonation — An explosion or sudden report made by the near-instantaneous decomposition or combustion of unstable substances.

Dynamite — A class of powerful explosives composed of nitroglycerin or ammonium nitrate dispersed in an absorbent medium with a combustible dope, such as wood pulp, and an antacid, such as calcium carbonate.

Explosives — A substance that contains a great amount of stored energy that can produce an explosion, a sudden expansion of the material after initiation, usually accompanied by the production of light, heat, sound, and pressure.

Fuse — A mechanical or electronic device for initiating munitions, such as bombs, shells, and mines.

Hot zone — The area that immediately surrounds the location of an explosive blast.

Improvised explosive device (IED) — A homemade bomb constructed and deployed in ways other than in conventional military action.

Incendiary — Bombs or bomb-making materials designed to start fires.

Munitions — Often defined as a synonym for ammunition, a narrower definition would include bombs, missiles, warheads, and mines.

Perimeter — The boundary of a crime scene.

Pipe bomb — An improvised explosive device manufactured by tightly sealing a section of pipe that is filled with an explosive material. The containment provided by the pipe allows simple low explosives to produce a relatively large explosion, and the fragmentation of the pipe itself creates potentially lethal shrapnel.

Plastic explosive — A specialized form of explosive material that consists of soft and hand-moldable solid material. Common plastic explosives include Semtex and C-4. Plastic explosives are especially suited for explosive demolition because they can be easily formed into the best shapes for cutting structural members, and have a high enough velocity of detonation and density for metal cutting work.

Secondary device — Devices designed to activate after a primary device (such as a bomb) with the goal of killing or injuring first responders.

Shaped charge — An explosive charge shaped to focus the effect of an explosive's energy. Various types are used to cut and form metal, to initiate nuclear weapons, or to penetrate armor. A typical modern lined shaped charge can penetrate armor steel to a depth of seven or more times the diameter of the charge's cone.

Shrapnel — Materials that are produced from a bomb, shell, or mine fragments.

Trinitrotoluene — Commonly known and abbreviated as TNT, this is a chemical compound with the formula $C_6H_2(NO_2)_3CH_3$. This yellow-colored solid is sometimes used as a reagent in chemical synthesis, but it is best known as a useful explosive material with convenient handling properties. The explosive yield of TNT is considered to be the standard measure of strength of bombs and other explosives.

MODULE 5

Emergency Incidents & Procedures

Key Module Concepts:

- The initial goals of the officer responding to an emergency

- Steps to securing a large-scale emergency of any type

- Additional responsibilities of officers and response teams during a large-scale emergency

- Identifying an incident as a HAZMAT emergency

- Defining and extinguishing the four major classes of fire

Introduction

Patrol officers respond to many types of calls. Nearly all calls for service are emergencies, but many of those emergencies become fairly routine situations for officers. In this Module, we will discuss serious emergencies, such as hazardous materials (HAZMAT) incidents and fires, which result in injuries and loss of life.

You will learn that most HAZMAT incidents are due to spills or leaks of dangerous industrial substances while they are transported across the country on our highways or railways. You will learn how to identify when and what type of hazardous material is involved in an emergency, as well as basic fire safety precautions.

In all such emergencies, you will need the help of other officers, agencies and professionals. We will consider how to get this help on scene as quickly as possible.

This Module is not designed to make you a HAZMAT professional or a firefighter. It is designed to keep you safe when you are a first responder to these types of emergencies. Your safety in large-scale emergencies is key.

Large-scale emergencies will seem overwhelming initially, but if handled in a safe, calm manner with some forethought, they will go as smoothly as can be expected for a disaster situation.

Ask Yourself

- *What would you do if you were the first responder to a commercial 767 crash in a residential area of your city?*

- *How would you handle a large building collapse after a hurricane, tornado, or earthquake when there is no power?*

- *As a first responder, how would you handle a HAZMAT emergency? Who would you call for help?*

- *What would you do if you were the first responder to a large apartment fire with victims trapped inside?*

Emergency Incidents

Every call to 911 is an emergency to someone. Loud music, a barking dog, or a cat in a tree is not an emergency to the responding officer, but the officer must take some action because it is an emergency to the person who called for assistance. However, in true emergencies, action must be taken to save lives or mitigate the situation. These actions might involve emergencies such as a car crash with injuries; a commercial transportation accident, such as a plane crash; a house fire; a building collapse after a hurricane or tornado; an explosion; a hazardous chemical spill or a terrorist attack.

Major emergencies are relatively rare in the daily routine of officers and security personnel. However, large-scale emergencies and disasters share many similarities with smaller, more common emergencies. In both cases, there are protocols to be followed in the immediate period following the emergency, although there may be additional problems and resulting procedures in large-scale situations.

Large-scale emergencies may deplete local resources, and consequently the on-duty officer may be faced with an overwhelming workload until off-duty personnel can be called in to help. Sometimes citizens will be able to help, or volunteer groups may be mobilized, such as explorer scouts or reserve officers. Depending upon the incident, state or federal resources, such as the National Guard or federal disaster assistance teams, may be called upon. Non-government organizations, such as the Red Cross and the Salvation Army, might also be available. Churches and other organizations may be of assistance as well. Though each of these additional resources offer help in a large-scale emergency, they can require significant amounts of time to arrive and get organized. As the original on-duty officer, what do you do while help is on the way?

First Responder Responsibilities

The first responders at an emergency may be police officers, firefighters, or paramedics. Some areas in the U.S. even have **certified first responders (CFRs)**, who are trained in responding to emergencies. CFRs have some medical training and will be able to help with the injured, but CFRs are not in place everywhere in the U.S. If you have them in your area, meet with them before an emergency occurs to learn what they can do to assist you, and how to activate them when necessary.

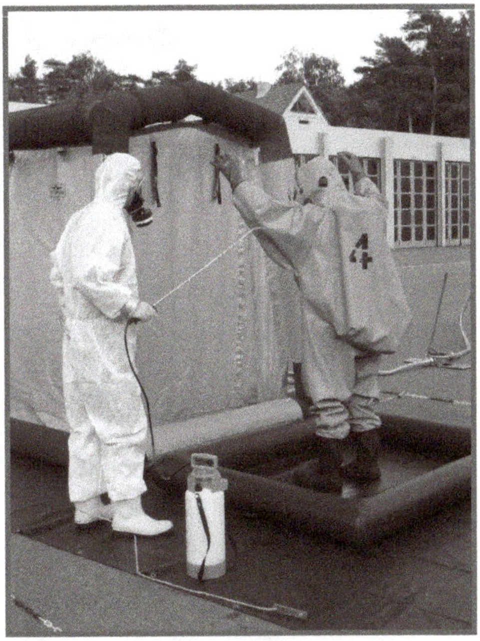

Your first responsibility as a first responder is to keep yourself safe. If you are injured, you cannot help, and you will utilize more emergency resources that need to be freed up to help the initial victims. Make sure the scene is safe for yourself and for other emergency responders before you enter. If the emergency appears to be the work of terrorists, be aware that there may be secondary devices on site. Look for these devices and observe any suspicious activity of spectators at the scene. Wear your **personal protective equipment**, which is designed for personal safety, into the scene. At the minimum, gloves

FIGURE 5.1: *Wearing personal protective equipment helps to keep first responders safe from the environmental hazards of an emergency.*

should be worn; if you are carrying a mask and full-body **bunny suit** to protect clothing, be sure to wear them. If you have a respirator mask that filters better than a typical mask, wear that instead.

As the first responder, you should size up the scene quickly and call for backup, such as other officers, firefighters, and medical personnel. You should also have dispatch notify the local dispatch notify the local emergency rooms about the disaster if it seems likely there will be a large number of injured victims.

If there are any suspicions of chemical or biological materials, or radiation involved in the emergency, HAZMAT teams must be called to identify the hazards and determine the level of protective gear required within the scene. A site must be designated for the dispersal and **donning** (putting on) of the gear. Decontamination stations should be set up where personnel can **doff**, or remove, contaminated gear and decontaminate themselves before exiting the scene. There may also need to be a site to decontaminate vehicles leaving the scene, depending upon the suspected or known contaminants in the scene.

Most emergency rooms in the post-9/11 era have decontamination teams. If the disaster appears to involve any kind of hazardous materials, the emergency room personnel must know this so they can set up their decontamination equipment in order to help victims. Patients contaminated by chemicals or radiation who are taken directly into the ER may, in turn, contaminate that area, rendering the entire ER unsafe and resulting in its closure. If a large number of injured people are anticipated, the ER staff may be able to set up temporary sites to treat patients at or near the scene; this will minimize traffic flow from the scene to the various ERs. Mobile command posts can be brought to the scene, and commanders can be identified to organize the initial emergency response.

If other officers are at the scene with you, begin organizing yourselves, leaving some officers to secure the scene. Identify safe ingress and egress areas where there is minimal debris and evidence. Quickly collect any evidence in these areas.

The **ingress** area is where other emergency personnel and vehicles may enter the scene. Have someone keep a list of all personnel who enter the scene. This person should also ensure that untrained volunteers who may hurt the victims, destroy evidence, or hurt themselves are not admitted. The personnel in charge of the ingress area also keeps media personnel out, and filters out terrorists who may be intent on injuring or killing first responders to stop rescue efforts.

The **egress** area is where the emergency personnel and vehicles exit the scene. Have a separate person keep a list of personnel leaving the scene. These lists are very important safeguards. If any personnel are reported missing, you must know if they safely left the scene, or if they may be trapped or injured inside the scene. In very large scenes, there may be multiple ingress and egress sites, and lists must be kept at all these sites. For example, the World Trade Center scene after 9/11 was 16 acres in size; each site in that 16 acres needed its own ingress and egress list.

The large scale emergency scene will be chaotic. If there are victims who need to be rescued or moved to a safer area, begin this process. If emergency medical personnel arrive, work as a team to rescue or move victims. Identify a safe location where victims will gather, and move injured victims to this location. When possible, have officers collect demographic information and statements from the victims who are able to give this information.

When moving injured victims, remember that basic first aid skills and CPR may be needed. Apply pressure to sites that are bleeding freely. Stabilize the neck and back before moving anyone, in case that person has a broken neck or back. Position the victim so that the airway is open so he can breathe. Alert medical personnel immediately if you find a victim who appears to be critically injured or who may be dead. Begin CPR and basic first aid until medical personnel arrive. These steps are all taken nearly simultaneously.

It is also imperative to search for both a cause and perpetrator of the emergency. In some cases, the cause is immediately known and is not criminal. A tornado or hurricane can be predicted and still result in an emergency scene. In other situations, the cause of an emergency is unpredictable and unanticipated. There may be an explosion or a fire, a train derailment or a large airliner crash. It is best to handle the sites of such emergencies as crime scenes until proven otherwise. The integrity of criminal evidence cannot be preserved after emergency personnel have contaminated a scene, so treating the area as a crime scene is appropriate. It is also best to make the initial perimeter of the potential crime scene much larger than is required; perimeters can be made smaller, but cannot be enlarged because anything outside the initial perimeter is subsequently contaminated.

While performing the basic steps in the immediate aftermath of the emergency, look for the perpetrator(s). Stop or confront suspicious vehicles and people. If you are busy helping the injured, call in a description or license plate number and ask for backup to try to apprehend the person(s) or vehicle(s). Give information on where the suspect or suspicious vehicle was located, and their apparent direction. Saving lives is a priority, but catching the responsible parties is also vital. Look for the perpetrator, but if you are busy with rescue efforts, ask for help in your search.

> **Resource** - Read about the initial moments after the World Trade Center attack from a report by the National Commission on Terrorist Attacks on the United States.
>
> **http://www.9-11commission.gov/report/911Report_Ch9.htm**

Additional Responsibilities

Local agencies have policies and procedures in place that must be followed in all emergencies. Consequently, other responsibilities must be fulfilled at a large emergency scene in addition to the previously outlined steps. The actual responsibilities met will depend on the size and type of emergency. Some are clearly law enforcement duties, while others may be carried out by members of other agencies or by volunteers, if necessary, depending on the time, manpower and resources available.

As previously discussed, treat all emergencies with an unknown cause as a crime until proven otherwise. The scene of an emergency must be processed like any other crime scene. Flag, photograph, and collect all evidence. Be alert for secondary devices or attacks, and alert backup about any evidence that suggests more attacks or devices. If the emergency is an explosion, the bomb squad must investigate and be notified of any suspected secondary devices. The fire department will deal with fires and explosions. The assistance of other law enforcement departments, such as SWAT, homicide and homeland security, may be required. Even if SWAT is not needed to force entry, having snipers oversee the operation to help protect first responders from another attacker is prudent.

Contact other agencies to help. There should be a disaster plan in place with **memorandums of understanding** (MOUs) previously signed to ensure that other agencies have agreed to help in a large-scale emergency. If there are obvious fatalities, contact the medical examiner or coroner's office immediately. Their staff may help the investigation by photographing, processing, and removing the deceased victims at the scene. If there are a large number of fatalities, they may choose to set up a temporary morgue.

FIGURE 5.2: *First responders work together to get emergencies under control.*

Ambulances will be needed for initial transport of the injured to the emergency rooms. A call should have already been placed to the local emergency rooms, and you should have information on whether or not a temporary medical site will be set up to treat the injured. Consult the local **emergency operations center** (EOC), which is designed to prepare for and coordinate in the case of large-scale emergencies. There should be plans in place for large-scale emergencies, including details such as when and where to contact the public transportation department to move victims with less critical injuries. Buses can easily transport these victims, leaving the ambulances for the severely injured. Buses may also be needed to evacuate people from the scene. Plans may include other details that are specific to a particular community.

Traffic control must be handled, sometimes extending for several miles from the scene. Traffic must be diverted away from the scene, keeping nearby roads clear for emergency vehicles. In large-scale emergencies, traffic control may be needed inside the perimeter. Pedestrians must be kept away from the emergency for several reasons: for their own safety, to prevent scene contamination, and to prevent secondary attacks from perpetrators intent on harming the first responders.

Areas outside the perimeter must be identified for both the media and the command post; these areas must be separated. A staging area will be needed for emergency vehicles to enter the scene. If possible, a temporary helipad should be located. Personnel should be stationed at ingress and egress areas as previously discussed.

Utility companies must be contacted. They must contain any leaking water or gas, and must begin power line and telephone line repair. Running water is important for decontamination. If there is no running water, water trucks and tanks must be available. Generators and lights should be brought into the site until the local power company is able to restore **grid electricity**. Additional radios, cell phones or other communication equipment may be needed on a temporary basis. When multiple agencies are involved in a large-scale emergency, English should be used in all communications, rather than numbers or 10-codes, because not all agencies have the same codes.

People may need to be evacuated for their safety. Teams must be arranged to notify citizens of the evacuation, and a plan followed to ensure that all people within the evacuation area are removed. Determine whether or not evacuees can take a personal vehicle out of the evacuation area, or if they must be bussed out or allowed to walk out of the area. Officers must keep the evacuees calm and prevent panic. A receiving evacuation area, such as a convention center, should be set up. The evacuation center must have enough food, water and toilet facilities for the expected number of evacuees. A medical clinic may be set up near the evacuation center for emergency medical care. The evacuees may not be injured, but may become ill with so many people in close contact with each other. Some evacuees who are on routine medications for chronic conditions may leave their homes in a hurry without their medicines, so medications may need to be dispensed to keep chronic diseases under control. If the emergency is going to be prolonged, local schools will often provide respite care, education, and activities to keep the children occupied. Local churches, civic organizations and even restaurants may supply and/or cook food for evacuees and emergency responders.

Counselors and local clergy should also be available. Victims, evacuees, and responders may have a difficult time psychologically processing the emergency, and having critical incident stress counselors on site is imperative to prevent long-term psychological problems such as posttraumatic stress disorder. The clergy members and counselors may also counsel families who have had a loved one killed in the emergency.

A public information officer (PIO) should keep media informed regarding new developments in the emergency aftermath, while an officer or commander should hold a variety of different briefings with victims, evacuees, and responders to provide the same information. Officers should obtain community demographics and conduct in-depth interviews with the victims to gain more information about what happened. Other officers should take data on missing persons. In large emergencies, command staff must work with the EOC to obtain help from other jurisdictions. If the emergency is overwhelming to local agencies, the command staff and EOC staff will work with the state governor to have a disaster declared so that federal disaster response teams can be mobilized to help.

Animals may have been injured in the emergency and need care, so veterinarians should be part of the emergency plan and should be contacted as necessary. Many people refuse to evacuate without their pets, so care or temporary housing may be necessary for pets. Depending on the emergency and its location, livestock may be impacted by the emergency, and may need to be rounded up and housed. Local wild animals could also create problems in some locations, posing a hazard to both responders and injured victims who have yet to be moved for medical care.

Each emergency is unique, and situations may arise without a clear-cut, ready-made solution. If you see a need, contact other personnel, dispatch, or commanders to inform them of the problem so that the appropriate personnel may be contacted.

HAZMAT Emergencies

Hazardous materials include agents associated with weapons of mass destruction (WMD), such as biological agents, chemical warfare agents, and radiation that is purposely dispersed in a nuclear weapon or a "dirty" bomb. There are everyday chemicals and radiation within our communities that, when mishandled or leaking, pose a HAZMAT emergency for those who come into contact with these materials. Hazardous materials are used in medicine and in industry, and they are often transported through our communities on trucks and trains. Even the gasoline we burn in our cars is a hazardous material if an unintentional spill occurs.

FIGURE 5.3: *Hazardous materials released by the terrorist attack on the World Trade Center on September 11, 2001 have caused death and disability among first responders years after the event.*

HAZMAT incidents pose special risks and dangers to first responders and to the public at large. As a first responder to such an incident, knowing what to do can save lives and prevent additional hazards. When you arrive at the scene, how do you recognize that hazardous materials may be involved? A large explosion may release hazardous gases, or may have been caused by a leak of explosive hazardous materials. A terrorist may set off an explosion to release a hazardous material, or may disperse hazardous materials in other ways. For example, the perpetrators of the 2001 anthrax scare used the U.S. mail to disperse a biological hazard in the form of a powder. A fire may release hazardous gases in the smoke. For instance, hazardous materials in the dust and smoke from the World Trade Center were inhaled by first responders on and after September 11, 2001. Many of those first responders currently suffer from disabling and, in some cases, permanent lung diseases from inhaling that dust and smoke; others have died from the complications of lung disease directly related to the WTC attack.

With the exception of powdered biological weapons that have a suspicious appearance, most biological agent attacks will not present initially as a large-scale emergency. The biological agent is usually a virus or bacteria. These organisms must be spread and ingested into the body; it can take hours or even days before the illness is manifested. Health care providers and emergency rooms will be exceptionally busy, similar to traffic during a natural disease outbreak. It takes time for health care providers to identify the disease and microbial agent, and then realize that diseases are the result of an intentional spread of infectious agents.

When a HAZMAT emergency is ongoing, the scene is divided into zones.

HAZMAT Zone	Description
Red Zone/Hot Zone	The most contaminated area; isolated from non-HAZMAT personnel. Only those with proper training and equipment may enter this zone.
Yellow Zone/Warm Zone	A transitional zone, where HAZMAT personnel don and doff their protective gear (in separate areas). Decontamination sites are set up in this area. Also called the *contamination reduction zone*.
Green Zone/Cold Zone	The area considered safe from HAZMAT contamination. Command posts, media and personnel resources are staged here.

Zones may change as conditions change; for instance, if the wind changes or an explosion occurs, zones may be shifted. Zone locations may also change as the hazardous situation is brought under control.

Risks and Outcomes Associated with HAZMAT Incidents

There are many potential risks associated with a hazardous materials emergency. One of the major risks occurs from exposure to the hazardous materials before their presence is known. The original call for service may be for a vehicle crash, explosion, or fire; the exposure to hazardous materials may be recognized only after the emergency response has begun.

HAZMAT emergencies may cause public health and environmental damage. There are both short- and long-term adverse health effects to humans and animals from these exposures, depending on the type of material and the level of exposure. There may be additional risks either from the material itself or from a combination of materials that are released; this combination can be even more dangerous than any of the materials on their own. An even more hazardous chemical may be created when the materials come in contact with air or water. There may be flooding associated with the leakage of material with resulting contamination of lakes, rivers, oceans, or local drinking water; therefore, first responders should remain upstream of contaminated water.

As a law enforcement officer, in the event of a suspected HAZMAT emergency, your primary responsibility is to preserve and protect life. You will typically not have the appropriate safety gear to enter a known HAZMAT scene. Much of this safety gear requires special training for proper use; it also requires annual fit testing to make sure it provides proper seals and safety for the individual who wears it. You must, however, learn how to recognize hazardous materials in order to contact HAZMAT teams; you must know the ways in which they will cause harm to protect others in the area before the HAZMAT teams arrive.

Distance is the key safety factor, so keep yourself and citizens far away from dangerous materials, particularly if they are potentially explosive. The scene may be even larger than the actual physical location of the emergency, due to the spread of hazardous fumes by the wind or by the risk of explosion, creating more of the problems previously discussed with large emergencies. Therefore, a large perimeter is vital in a HAZMAT incident. Evacuate people who are downwind of the emergency. As HAZMAT professionals arrive, they will test the air and advise you of the exact size of the perimeter of evacuation. Until you are advised, a larger perimeter is the safer bet. It is always better to evacuate more people than necessary, rather than to evacuate too few people, leaving some people in danger.

Different hazardous materials have different levels of toxicity or levels at which the material is dangerous. How damaging the material is to contaminated persons depends on how strong, or toxic, the material is, how much material was in contact with the person, and how long it was in contact with the person.

Hazardous materials can enter the body and contaminate it in many ways, including:

Avenue of Contamination	Method of Contamination	Preventative Measures and Precautions
Lungs (via nose and/or mouth)	Inhalation of gases, vapors, particles, fibers and biological agents such as bacteria and viruses	• Approach the scene from an upwind position • Wear a mask or other protection over the nose and mouth
Skin and eyes	Absorption through splashing, spilling or exposure of skin/eyes to gases and/or fumes	• Remain upwind of hazardous gases • Wash exposed skin surfaces with clean water as often as possible • Do not touch any potentially hazardous materials • Do not allow clothing or hands to touch your face or eyes

Avenue of Contamination	Method of Contamination	Preventative Measures and Precautions
Bloodstream	Absorption through skin puncture or open wound	• Be alert to scraping skin or puncturing flesh at the HAZMAT site • Leave the HAZMAT scene if you have an open wound of any size
Digestive tract	Ingestion through swallowing	• Do not eat or drink at or near a HAZMAT site • Do not smoke or chew tobacco near a HAZMAT site • Do not stick out your tongue or lick your lips at the scene of a HAZMAT emergency

The toxic effects of hazardous materials may be acute and occur within minutes to hours. These acute effects may occur with one exposure that is limited or short-term and may involve immediate burning, itching, or illness, and in a worst-case scenario, death.

The toxic effects may be chronic or create a distant effect. Typically, repeated or continuous exposures are required; however, a one-time exposure to certain levels or types of radiation may result in a chronic effect long after the exposure. These chronic effects may not be apparent for years. They include cancer, lung, and kidney problems that may result in eventual death. These effects may also cause repeated miscarriages and birth defects in the children of those exposed. Some hazardous materials, such as gasoline, can cause multiple effects. Gasoline is toxic and poisonous, may cause cancer, and may explode or cause a fire.

The toxic effects of hazardous materials will affect individuals differently. Children are smaller and lower to the ground than adults, so they will be more impacted by smaller amounts of hazardous materials or heavier-than-air gases. Age, gender, size, physical condition, overall health, and prior exposures to hazardous materials will also impact the outcome of a toxic contamination to a particular individual.

State and federal regulations attempt to protect first responders from exposure to hazardous materials. Exposures must be reported to employers, and those employers must keep appropriate records of those exposures for 30 years after termination of employment. Exposed first responders should also keep a record of all such incidents. Documentation includes the exposed person's name and the date, time, location and duration of the exposure, as well as the person's actions and duties at the location of exposure. It also includes the incident number and the names and concentration of the hazardous materials. The decontamination process and the medical treatment that was provided at the time of exposure should be noted. It may indicate ongoing medical treatment required as a result of the exposure.

First responders cannot refuse medical treatment for exposures. Federal and state regulations state that first responders must be evaluated medically if they are injured due to a hazardous materials exposure or experience any symptoms that are suspected to result from a possible exposure to hazardous materials.

Resources for a HAZMAT Event

There are many resources to help in a HAZMAT emergency, but the emergency must first be recognized as having a hazardous materials component. Hazardous materials at fixed facilities are identified by a warning system known as the NFPA 704 warning system. NFPA is the National Fire Protection Association; the NFPA 704 system consists of four diamonds that are grouped together to form one large diamond-shaped sign.

The diamonds are color coded for hazards:

- Blue pertains to health hazards if ingested; this information is located in the left diamond

- Red, the top diamond, pertains to flammability or the material's susceptibility to burning

- The right diamond is yellow, and refers to reactivity or the potential of the materials to react with other chemicals or to explode itself or become more dangerous

- The bottom diamond is white, and it is the area where special hazards are placed, such as radioactivity or reactivity with water

The degree of each hazard is numbered in a gradation between 0-4, with 0 representing no unusual hazard and 4 representing extreme hazard. The special hazard diamond will contain symbols to indicate the danger. For example, a line through a W indicates the material will react with water, and a radioactive symbol shows the presence of radioactive materials.

The **Emergency Response Guidebook** (ERG) is a book of symbols that are used as signs or placards on transport vehicles, tanks, drums and other containers, and pipelines. These signs or placards contain numbers and special markings that can be looked up in the ERG to see what is contained inside and the risk of the material. You should carry a copy of the ERG with you at all times on patrol.

R

Resource - This is a resource website that summarizes the approach to a HAZMAT scene for first responders. It includes a link to download the most current Emergency Response Guidebook.

http://www.ehso.com/EmergencyResponseOverall.htm

Material system data sheets (MSDS) are required to accompany all hazardous materials. These data sheets include details about the hazardous material in question, including safety, emergency, and decontamination information. If time permits, seek or ask about the MSDS about the material involved in the incident, because the MSDS contain accurate information and emergency response information about each specific hazardous material. MSDS are required to be at all sites that contain hazardous materials.

If a first responder discovers hazardous materials, the proper experts must be contacted. Notify the following parties:

- Dispatch
- The fire department
- The county health department
- The Office of Emergency Services

Notify all contacts of the location, type of premises or vehicles involved, the size and perimeter of the area, the weather conditions at the site, the type of hazardous materials, any sign or placard information including ID numbers and warnings, and safe entry and exit routes. Rescue personnel (EMS) must be notified, and a potential site for a command post set up, if possible.

Weapons of mass destruction (WMD) may be radiological, chemical, nuclear or biological. These weapons are also called **CBRN;** this stands for chemical, biological, radiological, or nuclear. If you suspect that a WMD has been used, contact the agencies previously listed. Any suspicious explosion may be a "dirty" bomb containing radiation. If you have concerns, contact the same agencies so that the site can be monitored to ascertain whether or not radiation is present. You should suspect biological weapons if a white powder is involved, or if large numbers of people become ill or die of similar symptoms. Suspect chemicals if there are similar symptoms in the victims and responders to an incident. These symptoms can vary, and include blistering, choking, and sudden death.

Safety Guidelines for First Responders

If you receive a call to report to a potential HAZMAT emergency, ask dispatch about the scene before responding. Ask about the size and location of the emergency, the occupancy type (if the emergency is in a building), descriptions of any vehicles involved, the weather conditions at the scene, including the wind speed and direction, possible number of victims, sign or placard information, identification numbers and warnings, where to meet the reporting party, and the safest approach route.

First responder safety priorities at a HAZMAT scene are represented as SIN, for *safety, isolation* and *notification.*

S is for safety. Keeping one's self safe means remaining a cautious distance from the emergency; approaching upwind, upstream, or from a higher point; and moving down toward the incident. *I* is for isolation, which refers to establishing a large perimeter around the incident to isolate it, keeping citizens and responders safe. Contaminated persons and equipment are isolated within the perimeter, but are taken to the safest place within the perimeter. *N* is for notification, and serves as a reminder to notify the proper HAZMAT personnel. Responding HAZMAT personnel are notified about the presence and location of the contaminated persons and equipment within the perimeter.

The Incident Command System (ICS), previously discussed in Module One, is used at a HAZMAT emergency. The incident commander will assume the control and management of the scene, becoming the temporary commander. First responders will report to the incident commander. State and federal laws require that a safety officer be designated at a HAZMAT scene. The safety officer will identify and evaluate the hazards, identify potentially unsafe situations, keep all operations safe, stop or prevent unsafe actions at the scene, and modify the response as needed to keep personnel safe as new hazards are perceived.

R

Resource - The ICS is used in large emergencies and fires as well as HAZMAT incidents. This Web site has an overview of the ICS, and a link for additional online training in ICS through FEMA.

http://www.fema.gov/emergency/nims/IncidentCommandSystem.shtm

---

CASE STUDY

Rural Arizona is an agricultural community where cotton, alfalfa, and potatoes are grown. Crop dusters spray chemicals on the crops for various reasons. Many of the crop duster planes are old biplanes fitted for use as crop dusters. The planes are heavy when filled with chemicals. The planes take a lot of force to swoop down low over the fields, and then climb rapidly to turn around and swoop back down.

One old biplane was dusting crops on a hot summer day in 1996. It sprayed a path through a field and then climbed rapidly. Witnesses stated that both wings simply fell off the plane during the rapid climb, and the plane crashed in the field.

Rescue personnel arrived to find a single pilot dead at the scene; no one else was injured. The chemical was an organochloride insecticide, which is a hazardous material. The tank containing the insecticide was ruptured, and the chemical was spread heavily all over the scene and the broken body of the pilot. The body was placed in a body bag and removed to the Medical Examiner's (ME) Office.

HAZMAT teams were called in to attempt to decontaminate the scene for the Federal Aviation Administration (FAA) personnel who had to investigate the crash. The field had to be made safe for future crops. Neighboring property, homes, and canals had to be kept safe.

The Medical Examiner's Office was told only that the victim was a crop duster pilot. When the body bag containing the pilot was removed for the special autopsy required on pilots by the FAA, the bag had an unusual chemical smell and appeared to be greasy. Calls were made to the police officers that had responded to the scene. The officers informed ME personnel at that time that the victim was killed in a plane crash later determined to be a HAZMAT scene, but they did not know what the chemical was, and were unaware of the decontamination methods needed.

ME personnel contacted local HAZMAT personnel, who were also unsure what to do, because they were not from the jurisdiction of the crash and did not know what chemical was involved. After many phone calls, the chemical name was identified, and ME personnel were told to flush the body bag with water, then remove the body and flush it with water until the smell was gone. The body was flushed with water that went into the local drain. No HAZMAT personnel responded to the ME's office to monitor the chemical concentrations. The chest had been crushed with open wounds into the chest cavity. No one could tell ME personnel how well the open chest cavity should be flushed. The autopsy was performed hours later than originally scheduled, with unknown risks to the environment and to ME personnel.

Along with notification of the proper authorities, any agency who receives potentially contaminated materials or evidence of any kind from a HAZMAT scene must be notified of what the contaminant is, how to decontaminate it, what precautions, if any, must be taken for the environment (for example, should water used for flushing go down the drain), and how to tell with certainty when the item is safe.

Fires

Fires need three basic elements to burn: fuel, oxygen, and heat. These three components work together to form a chemical reaction, known as oxidation, that causes fires. Without one of these elements, the fire cannot start. Removing one of these elements will extinguish the fire, so these elements will be important to consider again when we discuss extinguishing fire.

The fuel a fire needs can be solid, liquid, or gas. It is any combustible material that will burn. Some material must change form to be combustible; for example, many solids or liquids become gas or vaporize before they can burn.

The air we normally breathe is 21% oxygen. Fire needs oxygen to burn, but it needs a lower concentration to burn than we do to breathe. Fire can burn with as little as 16% oxygen, so even sealed buildings and containers can burn if they have enough oxygen.

Fire needs energy in the form of heat to burn. Heat is what often changes solids or liquids into a gas that will burn more easily. Gases will often ignite when they reach a high enough temperature.

Patrol officers need to know some basic information about fires because they may be called upon to respond to a 911 call involving a fire. Firefighters will likely be on scene before or shortly after dispatched officers. They will typically have an assigned safety officer, and they will assist in all of the topics discussed in this section. Always ask available fire personnel on scene before taking any action regarding the fire.

Classes of Fires and Indicators for Unsafe Entry into a Fire

There are four classes of fires:

- A **Class A** fire is composed of ordinary combustible materials such as cloth, wood, rubber, paper, or some plastics

- A **Class B** fire is composed of combustible or flammable liquids like kerosene, paint, gasoline, propane, and paint thinners

- A **Class C** fire is an electrical fire due to energized electrical equipment like faulty appliances, electrical panel boxes, power tools, or switches

- A **Class D** fire is due to combustible metals that burn at high temperatures that also give off enough oxygen to support combustion. These metals include potassium, sodium, titanium, and magnesium. These metals may react violently with water or other chemicals, so you cannot extinguish them with water.

The fire scene is unsafe for patrol officers who do not have appropriate personal safety gear designed for fire entry. Additionally, if the fire is spreading rapidly, it is unsafe to enter. If you see that living people are trapped inside a structure that is unsafe for you to enter, radio fire personnel

of the victims' locations and your location, so firefighters can enter the scene. They have proper safety gear for entry, as well as training on how to get victims safely out of the fire. Even so, entering the burning structure is dangerous, even for trained firefighters.

FIGURE 5.4: *Law enforcement officers who have been dispatched to the scene of a fire should always ask firefighters before taking any action regarding that fire.*

Principles of Searching a Burned Building

If a burned building needs to be searched, the fire safety officer will notify you when it is safe to enter the building. The safety officer will ensure that the fire is out, and that the structural elements are cool enough to allow entry. He/she will also assess that the building is structurally sound to enter. This means that the building will not collapse from above, and that the floor can support the weight of the search party. The safety officer will also tell you what kind of safety gear you must wear to enter the burned building. If you do not have the proper safety attire to enter the building, you must borrow it from resting firefighters or have another officer bring it to you. You cannot enter the building, under any circumstances, unless you are dressed appropriately as per the fire safety officer. You cannot enter the building wearing safety gear that does not fit properly, or that you have not been trained or fit tested to use.

Once you have the proper safety equipment and enter the building, be aware of the hazards inside. In the immediate aftermath of a fire, burned buildings are usually wet and slippery inside. There will be sharp objects consisting of broken glass and protruding nails. Your vision may be obstructed by safety gear, and your footing may be clumsy because of boots. Boards and flooring may be uneven. Trip hazards are present. There may be low-hanging boards or parts of the ceiling or roof that have fallen. You may uncover portions of the burned building that are still hot enough to cause burns.

Fire personnel will usually take you into the burned building and show you where to walk. If they suspect arson, they will tell you what should not be touched and explain why they suspect arson. If the fire is not suspected to be arson, fire personnel will show you what they think caused the fire. The fire arson investigators usually perform their own search, but if you have entered to assist their search, they will show you where to search and describe to you what you are looking for.

Fire is a common way to try to hide evidence of a homicide. You may start looking for homicide evidence, if, for example, firefighters have found a body that was clearly shot or stabbed before the fire. Fire personnel will have entered and looked over the scene before they allow you to enter, and will show you where they think the most suspicious evidence will be. You may photograph and collect the evidence upon approval of fire personnel. If you want your crime scene technicians to enter the scene, ask fire personnel for permission before your team enters the building. It is prudent to work through the burned building using the buddy system, so that you are always with a partner in the burned building in case one of you gets into some kind of trouble and requires help.

Extinguishing Fire, Hazards of Burning Structures, and Securing the Fire Scene

If the fire is small and has not spread from its original starting point, you may try to extinguish it. If you can attempt to extinguish the fire with your back to a safe exit, you may try to extinguish it. If you have the correct fire extinguisher, you may try to extinguish the fire. If none of these conditions exist, do not attempt to extinguish the fire.

Class A fires are extinguished by cooling the burning materials. This may be done with water. Class A extinguishers may be pressurized water or foam extinguishers, or a multipurpose dry chemical extinguisher labeled "ABC." Do not use a fire extinguisher labeled "BC" on a Class A fire. BC extinguishers contain carbon dioxide or a different type of dry chemical. As you extinguish a Class A fire, soak surrounding combustible materials to prevent the fire from reigniting.

Class B fires are extinguished by removing oxygen from the fire, inhibiting the chemical reaction that causes burning, or preventing the gases from contacting the source of ignition. This is done by using a BC fire extinguisher that contains either halon or carbon dioxide, a dry chemical which can make the fire worse. Halon is harmful to the environment, and is being phased out of use. Make sure there are no local laws against its use in your jurisdiction.

Class C (electrical) fires are extinguished by using any agent that is incapable of conducting an electrical current. Water cannot be used on an electrical fire. BC fire extinguishers are safe for class C fires. They contain carbon dioxide, halon, or dry chemicals.

Class D fires are extinguished by cooling the metal involved to a temperature below its ignition temperature, which is done using special extinguishing agents specific for the type of metal that is burning. This is usually a special type of dry chemical agent, although carbon dioxide or halon may also extinguish some of these fires. Halon and carbon dioxide leave fewer residues and are less corrosive on equipment that contains metal. If special combustible metals are present in industrial locations, the location likely has the proper fire extinguisher for the metals involved, but always make certain you have the proper extinguisher for any fire you are attempting to extinguish. Each fire extinguisher should be labeled by letter for the type of fire it will extinguish. Some are good for more than one type of fire and will be labeled ABC, AB, BC, and so on.

Fire extinguishers have a pin to prevent their inadvertent firing, or a "safety" similar to many firearms. **PASS** is the acronym to remember how to use a fire extinguisher. *P* means pull out the safety pin. *A* is for aiming the nozzle of the fire extinguisher at the lowest level of the fire or flame. *S* stands for squeezing the trigger. Hold the fire extinguisher upright while you squeeze. The last *S* stands for sweeping the fire extinguisher side to side while you spray the fire. Stop and leave the area if

- The extinguisher doesn't work
- The extinguisher runs out of fire retardant or water
- Your exit is threatened by fire
- You feel the area is no longer safe for any reason

Burning structures are very dangerous. Put your hand on a door before you try to open it. If it is hot, do not open, because the fire is near the door, and opening it may provide more oxygen to the fire, causing it to grow and spread. If you exit any area in a burning building, do not lock the door. You do not want to trap others who may be in the building, and you want the firefighters to be able to enter all doors when they enter the building in their safety gear. Use stairs to exit the building, rather than elevators. If you enter a stairwell, go downstairs. Heat rises as a physical property, and fire usually goes up also, so going down is always the safest route. Keep low to the floor to exit the building, because smoke and toxic gases rise; therefore, the cleanest air with the most oxygen is closest to the floor. Cover your nose and mouth with your sleeve or a cloth to keep smoke and particles out of your airway. A damp cloth is even better, if available. If you are trapped in a burning building, radio or use your cell phone to call for help and report your location in the building. If you are near a door that feels hot, do not open it, but try to seal the cracks under and around the door with clothing or any material that is available. If your clothing catches fire, stop, drop to the floor, and roll back and forth and around to extinguish your clothing. If you are with another victim whose clothing or hair catches fire, wrap the burning area with clothing, a rug, or a towel to rob the fire of oxygen.

Secure the fire scene with a large perimeter. As previously mentioned, the size of the perimeter should always be larger than needed. Nearby buildings can catch fire from heat on dry wood, from burning embers blowing on them, or from explosions, so plan ahead regarding your perimeter if buildings are close together at the fire scene. A rule of thumb is to make the perimeter at least as wide on all sides as the burning building is tall. This is to ensure that if the building collapses laterally while burning, the burning debris will be within your perimeter. This means if a two-story building is on fire, your scene perimeters should extend at least the distance of two stories in all directions around the base of the building. If a skyscraper is on fire, your perimeter will be huge. Secure the large perimeter and evacuate all persons within the perimeter. Do not allow evacuees or spectators to stand downwind of the fire, due to blowing smoke and embers, and keep them far away from all firefighting equipment.

As the officer on scene, you can help fire personnel by photographing the spectators frequently. If the fire is determined to be the result of arson, the arsonist is frequently in the crowd, eagerly watching the firefighting efforts. The arsonist may even attempt to assist at the scene in some way, so photograph everyone. Let fire personnel know that you have taken the photos so they can contact you later to get copies of your photos if they need them.

Summary

This Module has discussed the similarities and differences in different types of emergencies, including large-scale emergencies, HAZMAT emergencies, and fires. Know what safety gear you have and wear it. Be aware of the special safety gear required for HAZMAT emergencies and fires. If you do not have the proper safety attire, do not attempt to get close to the scene. Your expertise is needed to secure the scene and the perimeter, to notify other professionals and agencies, to keep citizens out of the scene, and to control traffic. You may have to help with evacuations.

As a patrol officer, you may have different duties at different types of large emergencies. If the emergency is not a fire or HAZMAT scene, you can assist with rescue. Safety remains the greatest priority for you, for victims and for other responders. If backup is required, you must notify dispatch of the need for additional help at the scene.

Your ability to stay safe and to perform the tasks discussed in this Module will help keep citizens safe and calm, and will help to mitigate the emergency more quickly. Plans are usually in place regarding large emergencies, so know the plans, and know your agency's policies and procedures for handling these large emergencies.

Discussion Questions

1. What kinds of large-scale emergencies are most likely to occur in your community?

2. Discuss local buildings and resources that could be used in your community for a large-scale emergency (for example, a convention center for evacuees). Where is your local EOC?

3. Discuss actions to be taken by law enforcement at a large-scale emergency.

4. Discuss actions to be taken by law enforcement at a HAZMAT incident.

5. Discuss actions to be taken by law enforcement at a fire.

Key Terms

Bunny suit — A one-piece disposable suit, a form of PPE, designed to protect clothing; some bunny suits have feet to cover shoes and socks, and some have hoods to cover the back of the neck and hair.

Certified first responders: (CFRs) — persons who are trained in responding to emergencies.

Class A fire — A fire composed of ordinary combustible materials such as cloth, wood, rubber, paper, or some plastics.

Class B fire — A fire composed of combustible or flammable liquids like kerosene, paint, gasoline, propane, and paint thinners.

Class C fire — An electrical fire due to energized electrical equipment like faulty appliances, electrical panel boxes, power tools, or switches.

Class D fire — A fire due to combustible metals that burn at high temperatures and also give off enough oxygen to support combustion such as potassium, sodium, titanium, and magnesium; these metals may react violently with water or other chemicals, so they cannot be extinguished with water.

Doffing — The act of removing PPE or HAZMAT gear.

Donning — The act of putting on PPE or HAZMAT gear.

Egress — The exit location from a secure area.

Emergency operations center: (EOC) — A centralized management center for coordination of emergency activities in large emergencies and for planning and preparation for emergencies; separate from the incident command post.

Emergency Response Guidebook: (ERG) — A book containing all codes to interpret hazardous materials placards and signs to determine hazardous contents.

Grid electricity — Electricity transmitted from the power company through electrical lines.

Ingress — The entrance location to a secure area.

Material system data sheets (MSDS) — Documentation about a specific hazardous material that includes safety, emergency, and decontamination information.

Memorandums of understanding (MOU) — A prior agreement for agencies to work together under certain circumstances.

PASS — The acronym which acts as a reminder for proper fire extinguisher use: pull out the safety pin, aim the nozzle at the lowest level of the fire or flame, squeeze the trigger, and sweep the fire back and forth with the spray of the extinguisher contents.

Personal protective equipment (PPE) — Any equipment designed for personal safety, such as gloves, masks, gowns, face shields, etc.

SIN — The acronym for first responder safety priorities at a HAZMAT scene that stands for safety, isolation, and notification.

Weapons of mass destruction (WMD) — Weapons designed to create a large span of damage; they may be radioactive, biological, chemical, or explosive. Also known as CBRN (which stands for chemical, biological, radiological or nuclear).

MODULE 6
Alcohol-Related Calls & Civil Matters

Key Module Concepts:

- Recognize various indicators of intoxication

- Compare and contrast the intoxication indicators against possible medical condition symptoms

- Understand the definitions of civil laws and torts

- Mediate and keep the peace during landlord/tenant disputes, including the eviction process

- Explain vehicle repossession laws

- Apply an officer's responsibilities when dispatched to non-criminal matters

Introduction

A police officer or security specialist will respond to many calls that are not criminal in nature. A civil standby situation, a very typical type of call, usually requires an officer's presence to keep the peace. However, a civil standby can quickly become a public disturbance, violent confrontation, or other criminal offense.

Officers are also called upon to intervene and remedy situations involving persons who are intoxicated whose behavior may not rise to the level of a criminal offense.

To effectively carry out the duties of the job, officers must be able to quickly discern what is a criminal matter and what is a civil matter. Officers and security specialists must also be able to recognize when a situation that starts out as a civil matter evolves into a criminal offense, and be prepared to take appropriate action. When such a situation is resolved, the officer's observations, decision-making process, and actions must be documented accurately.

In this Module, we will discuss the common types of non-criminal calls for service and evaluate the options available to the responder. We will explore the other support systems and resources in the community that are available to law enforcement. The reader will explore information regarding intoxication identification, medical conditions that can display similar intoxication indicators, civil law, torts, landlord/tenant disputes, and other civil situations.

Ask Yourself

- *What are the indicators of an intoxicated person?*

- *If a person displays the indicators of intoxication, what are the responsibilities as the responding officer?*

- *How can one be certain the person is intoxicated? Are there other medical issues that could cause a person to appear intoxicated?*

Differentiating Between Civil And Criminal Matters

As an officer or security specialist patrols her assigned area, she may be dispatched to the scene of an incident that is not criminal in nature. Private matters often come to the attention of the authorities for several reasons:

- The participants believe that their private dispute constitutes a crime

- The participants believe that a crime may be committed during the process of settling their private matter

- Third parties witness a situation that they believe requires police attention

- Participants or third parties believe that it is in the best interests of all concerned to have an impartial authority figure in place to be a witness or maintain the peace

Crimes occur when someone breaks a statutory law or ordinance. If someone maliciously throws a rock through your window, that person probably committed the crime of criminal damage or vandalism.

Civil matters are disputes that do not constitute a crime. If a neighborhood kid accidently breaks your window with a baseball while playing in a neighboring backyard, a crime probably wasn't committed. That doesn't mean the neighbor kid's family isn't responsible for damages. That is a private matter and may be settled through insurance, small claims, or just a friendly agreement. However, if tempers flare while you and the neighbor are trying to arrange payment for the window, an officer may be requested by one of the parties to "keep the peace," although a crime hasn't been committed, and the situation is completely private in nature.

Calling an officer to keep the peace can often be a very reasonable solution that prevents a crime from occurring. By having an impartial figure of authority present, the elements of intimidation and anger can be kept in check.

Most officers would prefer to respond to a request to keep the peace than to a request to break up a neighborhood fight. This is why officers are often humorously referred to as the "ultimate social workers." They are at the scene working through problems with people before things get out of control.

Alcohol-Related Calls And Intoxicated Persons

While working patrol, especially during the evening hours, an officer may encounter people in varying degrees of intoxication. In some instances, intoxicated persons may be the source of the most activity occurring during the shift. It is also not uncommon to have to repeatedly deal with the same intoxicated person. While the calls themselves are common, each situation is different, and nothing can be taken for granted. Intoxicated persons can present a broad category of serious problems for themselves and others.

In today's society, alcohol can be consumed legally at home or at restaurants, parties, anniversaries, holidays, and sporting events. Being an intoxicated adult is not in and of itself a crime. Unfortunately, for some people, a transformation occurs when they drink that can result in negative consequences. When excessive amounts of alcohol are consumed, some people act in ways they would not act while sober. Sometimes, the intoxicated person's behavior comes to the attention of security or law enforcement.

Alcohol is a depressant, which means it slows the function of the central nervous system and brain activity. This can affect normal decision-making and can result in confusion. A person under the influence of alcohol may exhibit a variety of emotions ranging from happy to sad to angry and, at times, suicidal.

Imagine a scenario where a convenience store clerk calls the police and advises that a transient is "passed out" outside of her business. The clerk reports that the transient frequently comes into the store and purchases alcohol. The clerk is unsure if the transient purchased alcohol on this particular date; however, it is reported that the subject had been in the store earlier and was slurring his words. The clerk stated the transient appeared to be confused and was stumbling as he walked out the front door.

The indicators described by the clerk may lead one to assume that the transient perhaps drank too much alcohol and has passed out. One approach is to ignore the subject and take no action; after all, just being a drunk adult isn't a criminal offense. But is that the best choice? What if the person is sick or injured? Perhaps he is suffering from heat stroke, an illness, or dementia. One cannot make an assumption that the transient in our scenario has simply had too much to drink. Further investigation is required in this situation.

Determining Intoxication

How does an officer determine whether a person is intoxicated? There are a variety of common indicators to look for when determining if a person is under the influence of alcohol. First, simply ask the subject if he has been drinking. Be sure to record or document the verbal response. Frequently, he will confirm that he has been drinking, but may minimize the extent. Do not be surprised to discover very intoxicated people declaring that they only had one or two drinks. Obtaining an admission from the person who has been drinking is the first step in determining if the person is under the influence or has other problems. Keep in mind that just because a person is intoxicated doesn't mean he doesn't have other health or psychological problems. Again, further investigation is required.

Keep In Mind

Police officers who have a lot of experience dealing with intoxicated people who are operating a vehicle will tell you that the drivers will often say they have only had two drinks. This is often not the case! Violators will make every attempt to minimize their actual number of drinks, in hopes of persuading an officer that they are okay to continue on their way. Document their statement and continue to investigate.

Some individuals may be reluctant to admit that they consumed alcohol, out of concern or uncertainty as to whether they might be breaking the law. If an admission cannot be obtained, an officer must rely on their training and observation skills to determine if the person is intoxicated.

When someone has been drinking, she will typically have an odor of an alcoholic beverage on or about her person. Do not make the mistake of describing "an odor of alcohol" on the person, as alcohol is considered odorless. Always use the term "alcoholic beverage" to describe the odor detected. The odor of an alcoholic beverage or drink can be found on the breath of the typical intoxicated person, and possibly on the person's clothing.

The eyes are another indicator that a person may have been drinking alcohol. Alcohol dries the eyes, which can cause the tear ducts to work harder. The dryness irritates the eyes, which can also make the red blood vessels in the eye more prominent. When the eye is red and dry, the tear ducts work harder than normal to continually moisten the eye and stop the irritation. This can result in the person having noticeably red watery eyes.

Horizontal gaze nystagmus, or HGN, is the involuntary twitching of the eyes while the head faces forward and the eyes track an object that is moving from side to side. HGN twitching normally occurs at an angle greater than 45 degrees to either side. Under the influence of alcohol, this twitching occurs at a lesser angle, and a person under the influence of alcohol has difficulty smoothly tracking the object with his or her eyes. The HGN examination, when properly administered, is a strong indicator that a person has been drinking or is under the influence of alcohol. However, it is highly recommended that an officer be trained or certified in this technique before attempting to include it as a means of "making a case" against a subject.

Remember, alcohol is a depressant and can affect not only the eye movement, but also many of the other muscles and motor skills of the body. When a person consumes alcohol, her speech can become slurred. Alcohol can relax the muscles associated with the tongue, making it difficult for an intoxicated person to articulate clearly. By engaging the subject in conversation and asking her to respond verbally to elementary tasks, an officer can further evaluate the subject's possible level of intoxication.

Field sobriety tests (FSTs) are simple tasks that become increasingly difficult, if not impossible, to perform successfully while intoxicated. These tests include demonstrating the ability to walk a straight line, heel-to-toe, and balance on one leg. Inability to complete these activities is a strong indicator of intoxication.

Keep In Mind

When completing the field sobriety test (FST), you must place the suspect in a safe environment. As an example, an officer was performing a field sobriety test on a suspect in a parking lot. A vehicle entered the parking lot and struck the suspect. The officer was held responsible because the suspect was not placed in a safe environment before conducting the tests.

An officer must rely on training, observation skills, and senses in order to make an educated decision as to whether a person is intoxicated. Use a checklist to help identify and document intoxication indicators. Does the subject exhibit some or all of the following, and to what extent?

- Red, watery eyes
- Slurred speech
- Odor of an alcoholic beverage on or about their person
- Unable to maintain balance
- Admits to drinking alcohol
- Possible hazard to themselves or others

An intoxicated person is often unpredictable. He can be calm, collected, and even humorous one minute and then become irrational and violent in an instant. This creates an obvious safety concern for you (the officer), the intoxicated person, and the general public.

Once an intoxicated person has come to your attention, you become responsible for that person. An officer must ensure that any hazard created by the presence of an intoxicated person is properly remedied. This could range from seeking medical attention, getting assistance from a sober person willing to assume responsibility and custody, arranging for social services support, or even taking the person to jail for his own safety.

FIGURE 6.1: *Field sobriety tests are an invaluable tool for checking a person's intoxication status.*

When taking a subject into custody, or making an arrest, an officer must be able to articulate the elements of law that have been violated. The officer must also be prepared to defend an arrest decision if contested later in court. Most jurisdictions have specific laws regarding public intoxication. An officer must be able to determine that the offender has violated specific elements of the statute. Generally, those elements include the following:

- Subject is in a public place
- Subject has been drinking and is under the influence of alcohol
- The subject's behavior is disruptive (must be able to articulate the specific disruptive behavior)
- Subject is a danger/hazard to himself or others if not taken into custody

Medical Issues Can Resemble Intoxication

Alcohol slows the brain and muscle movement and impairs responsiveness; however, there are other medical causes that can have the same effect. It is important for the officer to make every effort to determine if the person is intoxicated or if he is suffering from a medical issue. The officer must rely on training, observations, and experience to determine whether immediate medical assistance is needed. A prompt and timely assessment can be crucial if, in fact, the person is truly in need of medical attention.

The following chart outlines a variety of medical conditions that may be confused with intoxication indicators.

Medical Condition	Medical Symptoms
Head Injury	• Impulsivity • Slurred speech • Paralysis of the extremities
Stroke	• Irregular breathing • Forgetful • Extremity numbness
Skull Fracture	• Slurred speech • Blurred vision • Vomiting
Transient Ischemic Attack	• Mini stroke • Inability to speak or slurred speech • Clumsiness • Hazy vision
Parkinson's Disease	• Memory loss • Aimless movement • Slurred speech
Multiple Sclerosis	• Irregular eye movement • Involuntary movements • Slurred speech • Unstable stance
Diabetes	• Increased urination • Dehydration, causing red eyes • Fatigue to stupor • Seizures

The conditions listed are serious and would require immediate medical attention. This highlights the level of responsibility placed on the officer. The officer must determine quickly if the person has a medical issue and arrange for immediate medical attention if that is the case. When in doubt, summon medical attention.

EXAMPLE: A city police officer was dispatched to a single vehicle accident. The driver, who was the only occupant of the vehicle, had veered off the road and stopped at the curb. The driver was a medical professional (doctor), and was dressed in hospital scrubs.

When the officer arrived, the driver was described as appearing disoriented and was trying to put the key in the ignition of the vehicle. The driver had apparently urinated on the sidewalk and had thrown up on his own clothes. The officer removed the driver from the vehicle and placed him in handcuffs. The driver's speech was "confused, thick, and slurred."

Two ambulances and crews responded and reported the driver's vital signs and blood sugar were normal. The driver submitted to two portable breath tests, both of which registered negative for the presence of alcohol. The police officer made the decision not to transport the driver by ambulance for continued medical evaluation.

The police officer had the doctor handcuffed and sitting on the curb when an associate, a nurse, drove by the scene and recognized the doctor handcuffed. The nurse stopped and made several medical observations. The doctor's pupils were "pinpoint and sluggish to react." The nurse demanded that the doctor be transported by ambulance immediately. This same nurse also had personal knowledge that the doctor had suffered a stroke in the past.

The doctor, driver of the single vehicle accident, was indeed suffering from another stroke.

Officer Responsibility

In the previous example, even though the driver displayed some of the indicators of intoxication, this officer may have rushed to judgment. There were other indicators that this was not an alcohol-related incident. The breath analyses indicated no alcohol detection, and there was no indication of an odor of an alcoholic beverage on or about the driver's person. There may have been other noticeable signs or indications that could have or should have been explored. Never rule out or ignore that there may be medical reasons for the type of behavior exhibited. It is important that officers always consider the possibility of medical issues rather than assume a person is intoxicated.

Intoxicated Juveniles

It is not unusual for officers to find themselves confronted with a group of drunken teenagers. In many states, being under the influence of alcohol when underage is a juvenile offense, and the individual may be turned over to their parents or referred to the juvenile court. The person providing alcohol for juveniles may also be subject to arrest. Make sure your investigation includes questioning as to the source of the alcohol in the juvenile's possession.

Juveniles often use poor judgment when estimating how much alcohol they can consume, and wind up as victims of crime or in the hospital being treated for acute alcohol poisoning. Some juveniles who under normal conditions would not engage in criminal activity may find themselves involved in a crime as part of a group or behind the wheel of a car.

If you encounter intoxicated teens, follow your agency policy and take action, whether in the form of an arrest or by turning them over to a responsible adult.

Intoxicated Young Adults

There are significant criminal, social, and financial consequences involved for young adults using alcohol irresponsibly. Although part of the youth population is legally allowed to purchase and consume alcohol, many of their friends and associates may be underage. Binge drinking at parties or events often results in a law enforcement or security response.

This information indicates that security and law enforcement have a valid concern when dealing with young people engaging in alcohol-related activities.

When responding to a call involving young drinkers, the officers must keep several things in mind:

- Have a clear understanding of state laws and local ordinances regarding alcohol use, possession, and distribution
- Identify any minors at the scene who may be in violation
- Identify any adults who may be providing alcohol to minors
- Identify and mitigate safety risks to participants within the confines of the law
- Seek support of any responsible referral agency or social services group when appropriate

Many resources are available through state and local agencies, as well as the National Institute on Alcohol Abuse and Alcoholism.

Civil Disputes

Police and security work is often associated with responding to violations of criminal law; however, a significant amount of time and resources are dedicated to dealing with civil disputes. The primary concern in dealing with civil dispute calls is "keeping the peace."

Keeping the peace simply means that the officer stands by and makes sure that individuals resolve their differences in a peaceful manner.

Civil disputes can escalate quickly and become criminal matters, depending on how the situation is handled. The officer must remain impartial and not get caught up in the emotion of the situation. The officer must also avoid giving advice other than directing the participants to contact their attorneys for questions regarding civil law.

In some cases, one of the participants may want to take action that constitutes a criminal offense. It is reasonable to warn the parties if a crime is about to be committed. The goal is to maintain the peace, let the participants settle their civil differences, and to react to any criminal offense which may emerge.

Did You Know?

During the early 19th century, civil and criminal trials were heard by the same judges. These cases were tried in the same courts. In the late 1800s, the State of New York began separating the two. Two different courts were established, with one handling civil cases and the other violations of criminal law. This successful structure in New York later carried over to other states, and eventually all states separated their judicial systems.

Financial Disputes

Many times, civil disputes involve financial matters, and one party desires a remedy of financial restitution from another. Examples of financially-related situations include: people complaining about the work performance of a contractor; auto repairs; repayment of a loan; medical malpractice and many other areas where a financial loss occurred. These cases may ultimately be settled in civil court.

At times, a simple request to keep the peace can be very challenging and requires special skills in diplomacy. It is very easy for the officer to become caught up in the emotional dynamics of a dispute, and it is often difficult not to take sides.

There can be an unrealistic expectation among the participants in a dispute that an officer knows exactly how to handle every legal issue and will be current and familiar with every criminal and civil law and regulation. This can be especially challenging in situations where emotions are highly charged and neither party is willing to listen to reason or respond rationally to the circumstances at hand.

A typical situation could involve a request to keep the peace over a personal loan between former friends. An officer may arrive having never met either party, but the people involved in the matter may expect the officer to immediately understand all of the nuances of the circumstances of the loan, and all of the civil laws and regulations surrounding this particular transaction. That expectation is not realistic or reasonable. The officer is only there to maintain the peace.

The officer needs to remain impartial, advise the parties to seek legal counsel if they can't work out the matter between themselves, and prevent any breach of the peace. In plain terms, the officer's job often boils down to preventing the two parties from physically fighting each other.

Some civil matters require the officer to resolve the situation in a more formal way, such as giving a referral to appropriate outside resources or recommending emergency restraining orders.

Landlord/Tenant Issues

Landlord/tenant issues are generally considered civil matters and should be handled accordingly. The police are often contacted when the owner of the home wants the occupant/renter removed, and the occupant refuses to leave or has not been given proper notice to vacate. Landlord/tenant disputes arise over issues that usually involve maintenance, rent increases, failure to pay rent, or damage to property. An officer will be called upon to keep the peace or mediate landlord/tenant disputes routinely during a career.

There are specific landlord/tenant laws in most states that outline the rules and remedies for these situations. Officers need to be familiar with these laws, but must remain impartial unless evidence of a crime exists.

CASE STUDY

An officer is called to a residence by the renter. When the officer arrives, the occupant explains to the officer that he has rented the residence for approximately two years and has always paid his rent on time. Recently, problems came up involving the plumbing. The renter explained that he has contacted the landlord about the problem over the last two months without result. Now there is no running water in the house.

The renter says that he did not pay the current rent, which was due one week ago. When he came home from work, he found the locks on the house had been changed, and the landlord had left a note on the door, ordering the renter to vacate immediately. The note also indicated that the landlord intended to seize the renter's property that was inside the house pending the full payment of rent.

Now the landlord arrives, and the two begin shouting at each other with anger that may escalate to a physical confrontation.

What steps should the officer take?

FIGURE 6.2: *The eviction process and subsequent legal action can be an emotional experience for both owner and tenant, so officers are needed to help keep the peace.*

In landlord/tenant disputes, it is the responsibility of the officer to ensure that no violence takes place. It is the responsibility of the property owner to go through the civil process to evict a tenant legally.

Many states have the same general rules, such as requiring property owners to give at least a 30-day notice to terminate tenancy. If the tenant does not move out, it is the responsibility of the property owner to begin a lawful eviction process.

The **eviction** process means that the owner of the property will seek a court order to have the tenant removed from the property. This process can take between 30 to 60 days. If the tenant appeals the eviction, the judge will hear both sides of the case and make a decision.

Tenants also have certain rights. For instance, in most states, a tenant's personal property cannot be seized from a rental home.

Now let's add another level of complexity. What if this occurred at a hotel? That involves another set of laws that an officer must be familiar with. The courts look differently at hotel stays because the hotel owner/customer relationship addresses a much shorter length of time. Hotel owners may be able to seize property of a customer if the person skips out on his hotel bill.

Officers are often called to stand by and serve an eviction notice. If an officer responds to this type of situation, the officer will need to understand and explain the eviction process to the parties involved, while also preserving the peace. In many cases, an explanation of the rules in an understandable way will encourage the landlord and tenant to act responsibly and within the law.

Properly processed eviction notices are usually handled and served by the sheriff's office that has jurisdiction in the particular location or county.

Narcotics-related activities that are conducted in a rented facility or residence are generally an exception when it comes to time limits on executing an eviction. Narcotics-related violations can expedite an eviction process in as few as three days.

Keep In Mind

Officers need to exercise particular caution and attention when responding to a landlord/tenant dispute that may involve the illicit manufacture of methamphetamine. Methamphetamine labs are potentially hazardous and explosive. This type of lab also creates a significant environmental cleanup hazard. If an officer suspects that a location has been an active methamphetamine lab, the best course of action is to vacate and secure the location, and request assistance.

Always remember that safety is the primary concern in these matters. That concern for safety extends beyond the responding officers to the involved parties and the general public that may be in close proximity. Intervening in a process that could potentially leave a person homeless can no doubt generate a wide host of emotions and unpredictable actions. Remain alert to all of the actions, comments, and movements of the involved parties. Follow procedure and stay focused.

Impounding a Vehicle

Impounding or towing a vehicle may seem simple enough, but as with many of an officer's routine duties, there can be a risk of liability if the process is not handled according to respective laws, local ordinances, and established agency policy.

FIGURE 6.3: *A vehicle may be impounded for a number of reasons.*

An officer may be authorized to tow or impound a vehicle for a variety of reasons. Some of the more common reasons are: the vehicle is incidental to a lawful arrest of the occupants; the vehicle is evidence in an investigation; or the vehicle is in violation of city ordinances, or creating a serious and imminent roadway hazard. Some more specific examples include: the operator is driving without a license; the driver was arrested and taken to jail; the vehicle was used during the commission of a crime; the vehicle is stolen and the owner can't come to the scene of the recovery or the vehicle is abandoned or parked illegally.

When a vehicle's operator/driver has been arrested, the vehicle and its contents then become the responsibility of the arresting officer, the arresting agency, or the private or governmental organization authorizing the tow. Some of the initial criteria to consider regarding disposition of that vehicle include the following:

- Can the vehicle remain at or near the arrest location?
- Can the vehicle be secured?
- Will the vehicle be safe if left?
- Can the vehicle be released to a third party or family member?
- What is the agency policy?

If the officer leaves the car, and it is broken into, stolen, or hit by another car, the officer and agency may be liable for damages.

An officer will have many demands on her time during a shift, and high-priority calls require an immediate response. Waiting for someone to pick up a car for an extended period of time isn't a practical or reasonable use of an officer's time. Officers generally decide after a reasonable amount of time to tow a vehicle rather than leave it abandoned.

When a law enforcement officer makes the decision to tow a vehicle, there are some protocols to follow. The protocols are for the officer's protection; they are in place to prevent false accusations and to avoid liability for the agency.

Some common complaints filed after a vehicle has been towed are the following:

- The officer caused damage to the vehicle, such as scratches, dents, and torn upholstery
- Items are missing from the interior of the vehicle (allegations of missing money, jewelry, and stereo equipment)
- The vehicle was illegally towed

Here are some ideas to minimize complaints when towing a vehicle. If the driver or owner is present, explain to that person the reasons you are towing the vehicle and provide him with information on how to get his vehicle back. If agency policy permits it, allow the driver or owner the option of having the vehicle towed or left in place. With either decision, also explain that he assumes responsibility for the vehicle, whether it is towed or left legally parked at a location. Be sure to document the conversation and the choice given by the responsible party. Always provide him with the tow company information, including where the vehicle will be stored. These steps can help to minimize complaints.

Vehicle Searches

Whenever a decision has been made to impound and tow a vehicle, an inventory search should be conducted. Most states allow for an inventory search of a vehicle without a search warrant prior to impound. An **inventory search** is allowed so that law enforcement can locate items of value and secure them for safekeeping until the owner can take possession of the items. A proper inventory search should document all the contents of the vehicle and become part of the official police report record. A thorough inventory search record serves to protect the property owner, the law enforcement agency, and the company responsible for towing and impounding the vehicle.

Particular care and attention should be taken when searching the vehicle to check under all seats, inside the glove box, under the floor mats, in the center console, door slots, map holders (on back of seats), any and all storage areas or compartments, and most importantly, the trunk.

If items are located that should reasonably be secured at the police station, those items should be accurately documented and photographed prior to removal.

As an added precautionary measure, and if able, the officer should take pictures of the exterior of the vehicle, as well as the interior, including the trunk prior to the vehicle being towed. If the owner files a claim or complaint that the officer damaged the vehicle, then the officer will be able to refer back to the pictures to prove the damage was already present prior to towing. On occasion, the tow company may accidentally damage the vehicle during the tow process. The pictures will also provide proof that there was no damage to the vehicle when it was turned over to the tow company. The pictures will provide evidence for the officer and agency in the event of a civil suit.

Pictures taken of the interior will show items or the absence of items left in a vehicle at the time it was towed. It is not unheard of for vehicle owners to claim expensive stereos were removed from their car while it was in police custody. Photographs can aid in identifying or verifying equipment that was or was not actually installed in a vehicle.

Summary

Officers are often dispatched to calls that are not criminal in nature in order to keep the peace and maintain order. Sometimes the situations become criminal offenses. The officers or security staff involved must remain impartial in the sometimes emotionally charged situations.

Officers must routinely deal with intoxicated persons. Officers cannot make assumptions about these individuals, and a thorough investigation of their circumstances and condition is critical. Some persons may, in fact, have medical or other conditions that have symptoms similar to intoxication.

In some cases, officers respond to private matters involving situations such as bad loans, landlord/tenant disputes, or disputes with contractors or mechanics. Again, the best path is an impartial stance.

Discussion Questions

1. How might a civil dispute develop into a criminal matter? How can a patrol officer take steps to prevent this from happening?

2. How is handling a potentially intoxicated adult different from handling a potentially intoxicated juvenile?

3. What are some indicators that a person is ill or otherwise physically compromised, rather than intoxicated? What steps should an officer take to prevent from confusing the two conditions?

4. How can an officer diffuse a financial dispute where both parties are asking the officer to act against the other?

5. What are some exceptions to the traditional eviction process?

Key Terms

Eviction — a court order obtained by the owner of a property to have the tenant removed from that property.

Field sobriety test (FST) — actions requested by law enforcement officers of people they suspect to be intoxicated, such as walking a straight line. When in a state of intoxication, these simple tasks can be difficult to complete.

Horizontal gaze nystagmus (HGN) — involuntary twitching of the eyes while the head faces forward and the eyes track an object that is moving from side to side. Normally occurs at an angle greater than 45 degrees.

Impounded vehicle — a car or other means of transportation that has been seized by law enforcement.

Inventory search — The process of searching, removing and documenting items of value from a vehicle that is about to be impounded. Search warrants are not required for inventory searches.

Tort — a civil wrong for which a remedy may be obtained.

MODULE 7
Applied Skills: Communication

Key Module Concepts:

- The importance of communication skills for law enforcement and security professionals

- The history and relevance of Terry Stops

- Field interviews and field interview techniques

- Media relations and the flow of information from law enforcement agencies to mass media

- The Miranda decision and its impact on law enforcement

Introduction

Communication skills are the most critical tools in the arsenals of law enforcement and security professionals. We use these skills on a daily basis. We question witnesses and interrogate suspects. We prepare reports that may be used to convict or to exonerate. Our reports can document or disprove safety hazards, mitigation efforts, and consequences.

Media relations are also an essential component of our professional communications. Criminal justice and security practitioners should understand the role of the media, know how to communicate their point effectively, and comprehend the strengths and weaknesses of different types of media.

Most of our day-to-day contacts are consensual, but many are not. It is important to know and understand the reasons for limits on police power, respect the civil rights of those who have been arrested or detained, and work within the law when conducting interviews and interrogations.

Ask Yourself

How can law enforcement and security professionals maximize their effectiveness in

- *Gathering information in the field?*

- *Communicating with mass media?*

- *Balancing effective interrogation with respect for suspects' civil rights?*

Field Interviews

An **interview** is intended to elicit relevant information from victims, suspects, witnesses, and other individuals. Effective interviewing is a critical skill for law enforcement and security professionals.

Field interviews are conducted outside the custodial setting, meaning that an interview is voluntary and the person being interviewed is not under arrest. They are generally conducted regarding a specific case or circumstance. The purpose of the interview is to elicit as much relevant information as possible to answer six critical questions:

- *Who?* Reporting party: victim, witnesses, suspects (names and descriptions) and other officers

- *What?* Type of offense or incident, property taken, damaged or recovered, evidence seized or collected

- *Where?* Location of offense or incident, perimeter established, position of victims, suspects, witnesses, officers, locations of property, evidence [gathered, seized or recovered], directions of travel, origin and length of skid marks

- *When?* Time of offense or incident, response time to scene, time of contact with suspects, witnesses and victims

- *Why?* Motive for crime or cause of accident, reasonable cause for stops and searches

- *How? Modus operandi* includes: vehicle weapons, tools, accomplices and disguises

Field interviews may be conducted as part of a criminal investigation, accident investigation (traffic, plane crash, natural gas explosion) investigation, or a workplace accident investigation (slip-and-fall, industrial accident, workers compensation). In some civil matters, such as neighborhood disputes or hearings related to police actions, interviews are also conducted.

Field interviews improve patrol officers' familiarity with the people on their beats; provide valuable suspect information to detectives; and provide resources for police and prosecutors involved in gang suppression, riot control, and other specialized fields. Information gleaned from interviews is usually incorporated into reports. Reports are a formal, written record of an investigation of a crime or other incident.

Field interviews may result from minor enforcement stops (such as noise complaints and littering). They may result from a traffic stop or **Terry stop**, which is a brief detention of a person by law enforcement officers, based on reasonable suspicion of criminal activity that falls short of reasonable cause to arrest. The Terry stop, or investigative detention, gets its name from a landmark Supreme Court case.

In *Terry v. Ohio*, 392 U.S. 1 (1968), the U.S. Supreme Court ruled that police may briefly detain individuals on the basis of reasonable suspicion of criminal activity. The Court further ruled that, in such circumstances, officers may conduct a cursory search of the person's outer clothing for weapons if they reasonably believe the person to be armed. Reasonable suspicion must be based on articulable circumstances, not a mere hunch. "Reasonable," as in other areas such as search, arrest, and use of force, depends on the totality of the circumstances.

On October 31, 1963, a veteran Cleveland police detective, working a downtown beat with which he was intimately familiar, spotted three unfamiliar men behaving in a manner that indicated they were casing a store for a robbery. Detective Martin McFadden (1901-1981) approached the trio, identified himself as a police officer, and began to question them. When McFadden asked one of the men (Terry) his name, he "mumbled something." McFadden then "spun him around" and frisked him, finding a revolver in his overcoat pocket. McFadden frisked the other two men, Chilton and Katz, and found a gun in Chilton's coat pocket. Terry and Chilton were arrested, tried, and convicted for carrying concealed weapons.

Terry and Chilton appealed their convictions to the Ohio Supreme Court on the basis of illegal search and seizure. In 1961, the U.S Supreme Court extended the exclusionary rule to all states; this rule, which grows out of the Fourth and Fourteenth Amendments, bars admission of illegally-obtained evidence into trial proceedings. An intermediate appellate court affirmed their convictions, and the state supreme court, citing a lack of Constitutional issues, denied certiorari. Terry and Chilton then appealed to the U.S. Supreme Court.

Writing for the majority, Chief Justice Earl Warren held that such detentions and searches, based upon "specific and articulable facts," were not unreasonable searches and seizures prohibited by the Fourth Amendment. As such, the U.S. Supreme Court upheld the convictions of Terry and Chilton. The Terry stop, as it came to be known, allowed officers to act on reasonable suspicion and conduct field interviews after identifying themselves."

Field Interview Cards

A **field interview card** typically is a pocket-size card, approximately 4" x 6." It provides spaces for the name, date of birth, address, school, occupation, scars, nicknames, tattoos, and gang affiliation of the person contacted. It can also document the names of anyone the subject may have been with at the time of the contact. It always includes a brief statement of the reason for the contact.

Field interview cards, which require less information than a police report, are used for a variety of situations. They are often used to document information about a person who is exhibiting specific behaviors that, taken individually or in combination, would lead a reasonable person in the officer's position to suspect that an individual is engaged in or plotting criminal activity. Modern technology can leverage the power of the field interview card by inputting the data into a searchable database.

Field Interview Techniques

Detective McFadden displayed admirable courage and deft handling of Chilton, Katz and Terry. His quick actions and reasonable investigative technique provided the legal groundwork for all future police contact with suspicious persons.

Approaching suspicious persons is one of the most routine activities in law enforcement, but one that can turn deadly quite rapidly. The suspicious person may have already formulated a plan for dealing with "nosy cops." Officers have to recognize and react quickly to threats that manifest during the course of the stop.

The field interview begins with the officer's assessment of terrain and circumstances, relative advantages and disadvantages, direction of approach, distance to initiate contact, cover and concealment, availability of backup, and other tactical considerations. If possible, the stop should not be initiated until backup is present or at least well on its way; this is especially true when confronting multiple subjects. Officers should use a "contact and cover" approach, in which one officer conducts the field interview while backup officers maintain vigilance over the subject(s) and surrounding area.

We should emphasize that any police officer may speak to anyone, at any time, for any reason. The subject of the officer's questions is at liberty to answer, refuse to answer, or walk away. It is only when the person is not at liberty to leave that Terry stops come into play.

Although the subject(s) of a field interview may be required to provide identification, that identification may be verbal in nature. With few exceptions (foreign nationals legally in the U.S., parolees, registered sex offenders), Americans are not required to carry identification unless they are operating a motor vehicle. However, private entities (for example, liquor stores, bars and movie theaters) can and frequently do require valid identification to enter or to transact business.

Officers should carefully document physical descriptors and identifying characteristics. They may also seek corroboration of the subject's identity by other means, such as a computer check for identification and physical features, an associate who is being questioned separately and out of earshot of the subject, an associated vehicle, or a bystander who may have cause to know or at least recognize the subject.

As in an actual interrogation, empathy and a calm, professional demeanor are powerful tools when conducting a field interview. The officer may be talking to a suspect, a victim, a witness, an innocent party who is now inconvenienced, or someone who is completely happy to talk to an officer. At the conclusion of the interview, thank subjects for their time and cooperation. Moral and Constitutional issues aside, it is just good business sense: respect yields cooperation, while fear and resentment yield silence and resistance.

A simple yet effective interviewing technique is the three-step approach. The technique allows you to establish rapport with your interviewee, filter extraneous information, draw out additional details, take careful notes, and verify the accuracy of what you have recorded. The three steps are:

- **Listen attentively**. Focus your full attention on your interviewee. Use clarifying questions, particularly **open-ended questions**, to elicit further detail. Be attentive to the differences between **facts**, **opinions**, and **conclusions** in the interviewee's statements.

When opinions or conclusions are offered, try to elicit facts that may substantiate them. You may allow the interviewee to ramble a bit at times before gently guiding him/her back to the subject at hand; this allows you to filter relevant facts from irrelevant ones. Be alert to non-verbal cues indicating untruthfulness or evasion; you may want to tease these out at some point in the interview, or you may want to make a note of the behavior as part of your report.

• **Take notes**. Ask your interviewee to repeat his statement while you take notes. You now have a sense of what the person is going to say and what information is relevant. Clarify any discrepancies or ambiguities.

• **Read the interviewee's statement back to him/her**. Ask the person to correct you if you have made any errors. Confirm salient points individually.

EXAMPLE: Palo Alto, California, found itself gripped in a decade-long reign of terror during the 1970s. An unknown man, who came to be known as "The College Terrace Rapist," was breaking into homes and raping women.

FIGURE 7.1: *The same skills that make an officer an effective interviewer can make him a good media liaison.*

College Terrace is a residential area of Palo Alto that borders the south end of the Stanford University campus. Many of the homes in the area are rented to Stanford students and alumni. Most of the rapist's victims were women in their 20s and 30s who lived alone.

In 1979, Palo Alto Police Detective Brian Vierra was combing through unsolved cases and realized that many of the rapes committed during the previous eight years were the work of one person. The *modus operandi* seldom varied; in addition to the target area and his preference in victims, the rapist would cut the phone lines and electricity into the house, enter through an open door or window, and cut the victim with a small knife before raping her.

Neighborhood watches were organized. The police established a nighttime command post in College Terrace. They even went so far as to put a female officer alone in a rented house, with instructions to leave the doors and windows unlocked, as bait.

On a summer night in 1980, rookie police officer John Costa responded to multiple calls of a suspicious person in the College Terrace area. Eventually Costa lured the man out of hiding. The suspect, Melvin Carter, admitted to prowling: "I know a lot of women here, not on a personal basis, and I felt like coming back for a visit." Prowling is a misdemeanor in California; since the offense was not committed in Costa's presence, and he had no identifiable victim to make a citizen's arrest, Costa was unable to take Carter into custody. Costa completed a field interview card before releasing Carter and turned the card over to Detective Vierra.

Vierra realized that Melvin Carter matched both the physical description of the College Terrace Rapist and the psychological profile worked up by a local psychiatrist. Detectives called on Carter at his place of work — information included on the field interview card. Carter gave them permission to search his office. They found 44 surgical gloves in his backpack, some stained with blood. Behind a filing cabinet, they found his knife and jumpsuit, as well as tools and lists of names and addresses of women he stalked.

Melvin Carter confessed to being the College Terrace Rapist. In fact, he confessed to more than 100 rapes in the San Francisco Bay Area, many of them unreported and many near college campuses. He even took police on driving tours to point out the scenes of his crimes. Police agencies closed unsolved rapes as far back as 1968.

In 1982, Carter pleaded no contest to 23 counts of rape, assault, burglary, and attempted burglary. He was sentenced to 25 years in prison, paroled after 12 1/2 years, and moved to upstate New York — near the SUNY Geneseo campus.

Detective Brian Vierra retired in the mid-1980s and now owns a private detective agency. Sergeant John Costa retired from the Palo Alto Police Department in 2009, after 30 years of distinguished service.

Media Relations

In the field of law enforcement, media relations are more important than ever. In addition to traditional media, the growth of New Media — blogs, social networks, and video sharing sites — means that information moves almost literally at the speed of light and in a decentralized fashion that avoids traditional gatekeepers. Different forms of media have different strengths, weaknesses, and techniques of which law enforcement and security professionals should be aware.

To effectively reach out to the public they serve, law enforcement must avoid the "control" mentality. We must accept that the public has the right to know what is done in their name, and that honest questions deserve honest answers. These goals can be met with a pro-active approach to media relations.

Media Relations law enforcement agencies are corporate bodies. Law enforcement agencies typically route their public statements through the chief or a designated spokesperson. Communications breakdowns and rumor mills occur in police agencies as much as anywhere else, so it only makes sense to have public statements made by the person who has the most complete and accurate information to convey.

Nonetheless, it does not hurt to be prepared to speak, either to the press or at a public meeting. Public speaking consistently ranks near the top among people's greatest fears. The officer who can speak to the public in a confident and articulate manner is a great asset to his or her department. Public speaking ability can, in fact, lead to career advancement opportunities. Joining Toastmasters, enrolling in a college class on rhetoric or debate, even acting in community theater productions, can help officers overcome "stage fright."

Effective press relations begin at the "pre-press" stage. This involves not just the media, but those who have the ear of the media, such as elected officials and community activists. Inviting them on ride-alongs and to squad briefings, training sessions, and community forums can help foster understanding and trust. Be prepared to listen and learn. When honest disagreements occur, as they will, the relationship built on these efforts lessens the chance of differences degenerating into mistrust and acrimony.

Effective press relations works to the advantage of both parties. Reporters always are on the lookout for stories, while police can use the press to inform the public of Amber Alerts, crime prevention tips, and other initiatives.

Managing The Flow Of Information

"Abandoning the control mentality" does not mean that press conferences should become chaotic. Any human interaction relies on certain rules, expressed or implied, to set the parties' expectations and minimize friction.

Russell Ruffin, an Emmy-award winning television news reporter who now teaches media relations to public safety agencies and private corporations, has some advice on managing the flow of information:

- Have a public information officer (PIO) conduct press briefings rather than the chief, sheriff, director, or other administrative figure. This minimizes the tendency of reporters to drift away from available facts and onto tangential or speculative questioning.

- Have regularly scheduled press conferences. Ruffin recommends every hour on the hour. Set the ground rules at the start of the conference (duration, protocol for submitting questions, etc.).

- Avoid negative statements like, "No comment," "I'm not going to give you that information," "Parents, stay away from the school or you'll be arrested." Instead, use positive phrases like, "I'll have that information for you as soon as it's available" and "Parents, please help us by avoiding the school and not making phone calls in to the school."

The **National Incident Management System** (**NIMS**) provides a framework for controlling the flow of information, particularly when multiple departments within a jurisdiction or multiple jurisdictions are involved.

Talking to the Media

Anyone engaged in talking to the media is the public face of his/her organization, and is in a position to make a profound impact on the public's perception of that organization. A 2001 study conducted by George Mason University on behalf of the International Association of Chiefs of Police (IACP) showed that the majority of the American public had favorable impressions of the police. The study also confirmed that a majority of the public got most of their information from mass media.

There are a few guidelines to keep in mind in talking to the media.

- **Be available**. Reporters usually operate on tight deadlines in order to be prepared for live coverage. Be on scene, or have a number where you can be reached. Return calls promptly, even if only to decline comment (remember to do so in a positive manner, as discussed previously).

- **Go for the sound-bite**. We live in a sound-bite age. Unless you are speaking with someone who is writing a book or a feature-length article, you may expect your comments to be trimmed. Distill your message down to its bare essence. Do not feel pressured into saying something you don't want to say, or to speculate on things you do not know about. At the same time, be sure you convey a genuine passion and enthusiasm for your work.

- **Know your reporters**. Even if you have no "official" media responsibilities, it is worth studying the reporters who cover the crime beat in your area. You will have a sense for their communication style, their personal biases and their overall knowledge of what you do. If thrust into a role as department or company spokesperson, being able to comment on a recent story of the reporter's can be a handy ice-breaker. Take some time to initiate contacts: a brief letter or email about a story, even a critical but respectful one, is always appreciated. Reporters need both an audience and credibility; you can provide both.

- **You are always on the record**. Even if you have a prior arrangement with a reporter, you should always consider yourself on the record. Reporters have a canon of ethics and generally will not reveal a source, but your remarks could become public in a different context. Be very careful about going "off-the-record" and about the things you say when you do.

- **Check facts and quotes**. Try to have a prior agreement with your reporter in order to get a prepublication draft of the article to check for accuracy. This applies to print media, including Internet text articles.

- **Expect the occasional inaccuracy or misquote**. Even the most conscientious reporters occasionally misinterpret something, which is why it is a good idea to read back statements to the people you have interviewed. Sometimes an editor may misconstrue a statement or attach a misleading headline or photo caption. A polite, professional correction is usually appreciated, and generally results in editing of an online article or publication of a correction for a print article.

Many of these same considerations will apply to you when speaking to the media. If you find you have made a gaffe, address it proactively. If a mistake is brought to your attention, deal with it honestly and forthrightly. Do not try to "spin" or "tap dance" around the issue, because your credibility is on the line.

FIGURE 7.2: *The ability to manage media relations is an invaluable skill for law enforcement officers.*

CASE STUDY

The Stuart, Fl., Police Department is proactive in its use of mass media, with benefits to the media outlets, the community, and the department.

The city of Stuart is the only incorporated city in Martin County, on Florida's Treasure Coast. The city has about 16,000 residents and is served by a police force of 46 sworn officers. The city is known as "The Sailfish Capital of the World," and is located in the 37th-largest media market in the United States.

One of Stuart's police officers is an avid long-distance bicycle racer who has earned many trophies in the sport. His off duty achievements have been publicized to the local media. As a result, he has been able to leverage his fame to secure the donation of hundreds of bicycles and bicycle helmets for children. The situation is a win-win, as the media has a recurring story, the community benefits and the department has a human face in its officer- athlete.

The Stuart Police Department makes extensive use of volunteers. It regularly reaches out to the media with profiles of those volunteers. Again, the media has a recurring story, the community learns more about their neighbors and their work at the police department, the department is humanized, and its volunteer program is promoted.

In addition to their mass-media outreach, the Police Department maintains an active Web site, which includes a daily log of police activity and press releases of significant events.

What can other police departments learn from the Stuart Police Department?

Miranda Rights

According to the Fifth Amendment of the U.S. Constitution, "No person shall be held to answer for a capital, or otherwise infamous crime, unless on a presentment or indictment of a Grand Jury, except in cases arising in the land or naval forces, or in the Militia, when in actual service in time of War or public danger; nor shall any person be subject for the same offense to be twice put in jeopardy of life or limb; **_nor shall be compelled in any criminal case to be a witness against himself_**, nor be deprived of life, liberty, or property, without due process of law; nor shall private property be taken for public use, without just compensation."

In 1963, Phoenix resident Ernesto Miranda was picked up by police as a suspect in the kidnapping and rape of an 18-year old woman. Miranda was interrogated for two hours before he confessed to the charges. He had no counsel present and was informed neither of his right to remain silent nor of his right to counsel. Miranda was convicted solely on the basis of his confession and sentenced to 20 to 30 years in prison.

Miranda appealed his conviction to the Arizona Supreme Court, arguing that his confession had been unconstitutionally obtained. The court upheld the conviction, whereupon Miranda appealed to the U.S. Supreme Court, which heard the case in 1966. In a 5-4 decision, the U.S. Supreme Court ruled that Miranda's Constitutional rights had been violated and that his confession was inadmissible as evidence.

Writing for the majority, Chief Justice Earl Warren held that Miranda's rights against self-incrimination and to legal counsel had been violated. In addition to the legal precedents, Warren cited both FBI procedures and the Uniform Code of Military Justice, which required that suspects be informed of their right to remain silent; the FBI manual also required that suspects be informed of their right to counsel. The Court asserted a stunning, procedural standard to be followed:

"[T]he prosecution may not use statements...stemming from custodial interrogation of the defendant unless it demonstrates the use of procedural safeguards effective to secure the privilege against self-incrimination. Custodial interrogation is initiated by law enforcement after a person has been taken into custody or otherwise deprived of his freedom of movement.

... Before any questioning, the person must be warned that he has a right to remain silent, that any statement he does make may be used as evidence against him, and that he has a right to the presence of an attorney, either retained or appointed."

The Warren Court, already controversial, drew even more ire from police and politicians. Many predicted the end of the use of confessions in crime fighting. Richard Nixon, campaigning for President in 1968, blamed the Supreme Court's decisions in Miranda and other, similar cases for the country's rising crime rate. In fact, the decision had little, if any, impact on the ability of the police to solve crimes.

Movies and television shows quickly adapted to the new procedures. The image of police reading a suspect his Miranda rights became a regular sight in film and TV shows, and many aficionados of crime drama soon found they had memorized the admonishment themselves.

Miranda in the Field

The Miranda Card has become a standard issue item for law enforcement officers. A typical Miranda Card reads as follows:

- You have the right to remain silent

- If you give up that right, anything you say can and will be used against you in a court of law

- You have the right to an attorney and to have an attorney present during questioning

- If you cannot afford an attorney, one will be provided to you at no cost

- During any questioning, you may decide at any time to exercise these rights, not answer any questions or make any statements

- Do you understand each of these rights as I have read them to you?

Suspects may waive their rights under Miranda. The courts require that three conditions be fulfilled for any such waiver.

- The waiver must be *knowing*. The suspect must know that he has rights against self-incrimination and to the presence of an attorney during questioning, and that he is waiving those rights.

- The waiver must be *intelligent*. The suspect must know and understand the implications of waiving his rights.

- The waiver must be *voluntary*. The waiver cannot have been obtained through physical or psychological coercion, threats, or promises of lenient treatment or other reward.

Because of the burden of proof placed on the police by the Warren Court, many departments require an affirmative acknowledgment of each item as it is being read.

In examining the requirements of the Miranda decision, it is helpful to break down the elements of law, just as we would articulate the elements of law in writing a crime report.

The evidence must have been gathered. This is the starting point of all rules of evidence; there is no arguing evidence that exists only in theory, if at all.

The evidence must be testimonial. Miranda covers only **testimonial evidence** — communication, explicit or implicit, meant to convey a fact, belief, or other information. The communication may be verbal or non-verbal. Suspects may be compelled to give physical evidence, such as DNA samples, blood specimens and dental impressions. Although not subject to Miranda, such compulsion will have implications under Fourth Amendment search and seizure protections, as well as laws and policies relating to use of force, which the investigating officer must recognize.

The evidence must have been gathered while the suspect was in custody. The suspect, must know, or reasonably believe, that he is under arrest. Physical restraint is not necessary; simply telling the suspect "You are under arrest" is sufficient. A brief stop, such as a traffic stop or a Terry stop, even though the person stopped is not at liberty to leave, does not constitute an arrest requiring Miranda prior to questioning. Officers may not, however, detain a person longer than is reasonably necessary to accomplish the purpose of the stop (for example, issuing a traffic citation).

The evidence must have been the product of interrogation. Generally, with the exception of minors, there is no requirement to read Miranda immediately upon arrest. **Interrogation** is questioning intended to elicit a confession or evidence of a crime. Questioning incidental to the arrest (name, date of birth, address, occupation) does not constitute interrogation. Spontaneous statements are allowed (at least prior to *Berghuis v. Thompkins*) but may not constitute a waiver of rights with respect to interrogation. In *New York v Quarles* (1984), the court crafted a "public safety" exemption to Miranda, allowing the admission of evidence from un-Mirandized interrogation when such interrogation is necessary to prevent imminent harm.

The interrogation must have been conducted by state agents. Miranda is intended as a check on governmental despotism. It does not apply to private parties, such as private security officers, though it may apply to off-duty police officers moonlighting as security officers. Statements made when the suspect is unaware that he is talking to a **state agent** (police informant, undercover officer, etc.) are considered freely given and not covered by Miranda.

The evidence must be offered by the state in the course of a criminal prosecution. This goes almost without saying: there is no debating the admissibility of evidence unless it first is offered. However, law enforcement officers should be aware that evidence obtained pursuant to an illegal interrogation may be ruled inadmissible as "fruit of the poisoned tree."

In *Berghuis v. Thompkins* (2010), the Supreme Court considerably narrowed the scope of procedural protection under Miranda. By a 5-4 vote, the Court held that a suspect, informed of and understanding his Miranda rights, may be questioned until he explicitly invokes those rights. Essentially, the majority ruled that suspects, by their silence, give consent to continued questioning.

Example: In February of 1985, Robert Van Hook picked up David Self at a gay bar in Cincinnati, Ohio. The two men went to Self's apartment, where Van Hook murdered Self and stole a number of his valuables. Van Hook fled to Ft. Lauderdale, Florida, where he was arrested two months later.

Florida police read Van Hook his Miranda rights. Van Hook stated that he did not want to speak without counsel, whereupon Florida officers stopped questioning him.

When Cincinnati detectives arrived at the jail in Florida, they began by discussing routine items, such as extradition proceedings, with Van Hook. Unfortunately, although informed by the Florida officers that Van Hook had invoked his right to counsel, the Cincinnati detectives segued into a custodial interrogation. Van Hook confessed to the crime in detail.

An unsuccessful pre-trial motion was made to suppress the confession. Van Hook was convicted of capital murder and robbery by a three-judge panel in Ohio and sentenced to death. The district court denied his request for a hearing.

Van Hook filed a habeas corpus petition with the United States Court of Appeals for the Sixth Circuit. Although Van Hook raised a number of issues on appeal, the appellate court addressed only one in overturning his conviction: the admissibility of his confession. In *Edwards v. Arizona* (1981), the U.S. Supreme Court held that police cannot reinitiate interrogation of a suspect, even after re-admonishment of rights, once he has invoked his right to counsel.

The Sixth District reversed Van Hook's conviction and remanded the case to the State of Ohio for a new trial. Van Hook was again convicted and sentenced to death. His most recent appeal, alleging ineffective assistance of counsel at his second trial, was denied by the U.S. Supreme Court in December 2009.

Summary

Well-developed written and oral communication skills are invaluable to law enforcement and security professionals. These skills shape the public's perception of officers and their agencies while enabling them to get the information needed to prove cases in a court of law.

Contacts with the public may be consensual or non-consensual. In all circumstances, patrol officers must be mindful of the Constitutional rights of the individual, whether the subject is a victim, witness, suspect, reporter, or a person suffering from mental illness.

Contacts with the media can work to the mutual benefit of both the media and the law enforcement agency, as well as that of the general public. Be prepared. Know and understand the role and requirements of the different media. Consider how organization can take a more proactive role with media. If you have an idea, do not hesitate to send it up your chain of command.

Discussion Questions

1. Imagine a situation you might be called to investigate — a crime, an accident, suspicious persons or circumstances. What information would be important to obtain? What kind of questions would you ask?

2. Officers frequently deal with people experiencing extreme stress. How would you go about getting the information you need under such circumstances?

3. Are non-verbal cues important in interviewing? Would it ever be important to document them in a report?

4. Relationships with the media frequently are seen as adversarial. Why is this? Can these relations be managed to mutual benefit? Discuss.

5. Does the Supreme Court's decision in *Berghuis* significantly reduce the protections afforded by Miranda? Why or why not?

Key Terms

Coercion — Physical or psychological force, threats, or enticements intended to garner a specific result (for example, confession). Custodial situations are considered inherently coercive, giving rise to measures intended to protect the civil rights of suspects in custody.

Conclusion — A statement that is based on analysis of facts and opinions.

Custodial interrogation — Interrogation conducted by state agents known as such to the suspect, while the suspect is not at liberty to leave. The suspect need not be incarcerated or physically restrained. Statements made to undercover officers, jailhouse informants, and during the course of Terry stops, do not constitute "custodial interrogation."

Exclusionary rule — A judicial construct, dating back to English common law, which bars the admission in a court of law of evidence gathered by illegal means.

Fact — Something that tangibly exists; a statement that can be verified or proven.

Interview — A discussion intended to elicit facts or opinions.

Interrogation — Express questioning and "any words or actions on the part of the police (other than those normally attendant to arrest and custody) that the police should know are reasonably likely to elicit an incriminating response from the suspect." *Rhode Island v. Innis* (1980). Spontaneous statements made during the course of questioning "normally attendant to arrest and custody" are not considered products of interrogation.

Issue — Something about which there is a question or controversy.

Miranda rights — The right of criminal suspects to remain silent and to have an attorney present during custodial interrogation.

The National Incident Management System (NIMS) — A set of guidelines, established by the U.S. Department of Homeland Security, designed to improve preparation, coordination, and incident management in the event of a crisis.

Open-ended question — A question constructed to elicit a more detailed response than a simple "yes" or "no."

Opinion — A statement open to different interpretations and not necessarily supported by facts.

State agent — Anyone employed by or acting on the behalf of the government. This may include police officers, firefighters, police informants, and others.

Terry stop — A stop of a person, by law enforcement officers, based upon "reasonable suspicion" that the person may have been engaged in criminal activity.

Testimonial evidence — Communications, either verbal or non-verbal, intended to communicate a fact or belief.

MODULE 8
Medical Issues & Suspect Identification

Key Module Concepts:

- The ramifications of HIPAA

- The reporting requirements for suspected child or domestic abuse

- Procedures for ordering blood samples for use as evidence

- Strategies for obtaining good suspect descriptions

- The use of line-ups and suspect sketches in suspect identification

Introduction

Police officers spend a lot of time in hospitals. Whether it is to have a recently arrested suspect medically cleared before booking, to guard a convicted prisoner who is receiving needed medical care, or to interview victims or suspects who are patients, official duties put law enforcement personnel in contact with medical staff at various types of healthcare facilities. The different priorities of law enforcement and medical providers can easily lead to friction.

Since 2003, the **Health Insurance Portability Accountability Act** (HIPAA) has defined the minimum standards of privacy protection for patient information that all medical staff members are required to provide. Though there are specific exceptions, these rules are not automatically overcome by the investigational needs of law enforcement. In fact, divulging information inappropriately is itself a crime. Fortunately, the rules relating to law enforcement are straightforward and easy to understand. Therefore, it is still possible to perform investigations and gather evidence when hospitals are not allowed to assist.

Ask Yourself

- *When are hospital staff members not allowed to assist law enforcement with information?*

- *When are those same staff members required to report suspicions of criminal activity to law enforcement?*

- *How can an investigator get the best possible description from a willing witness?*

- *How is an effective lineup accomplished, and where do suspect sketches come from?*

Medical Issues

Police officers are used to being in charge. In order to be effective in emergency situations, they have to cultivate the ability to get to the root of the matter quickly. Scrupulously trained to remain within law and policy, they acutely feel the responsibility of providing the best service they can. They are passionate about their jobs because they know that lives can be lost if they fail.

Doctors and nurses are also used to being in charge. In order to be effective in emergency situations, they have to cultivate an ability to get to the root of the matter quickly. Scrupulously trained to remain within law and policy, they are still driven to solve the problems that are presented to them professionally on a daily basis, because they acutely feel the responsibility of providing the best service they can. They are passionate about their jobs because they know that lives can be lost if they fail.

What happens when the priorities of these two groups come into conflict? This happens far too often, but it need not happen at all. Just like every police agency has policies and procedures to be followed by every officer, so does every medical practice have policies and procedures for its employees.

HIPAA

Congress passed HIPAA in 1996, with most organizations required to be in full compliance with its provisions by 2003. It is a very complex and wide-ranging law. A main priority of HIPAA is providing continued health insurance coverage to workers and families when the worker loses or changes jobs. This is referred to as "portability." Title I of the law limits the ability of group insurance plans to place restrictions on coverage for pre-existing conditions, and also makes rules for how exclusionary periods are determined. An exclusionary period would be a length of time between when the worker began paying premiums and when certain coverage options were available.

Title II of the law was written to reduce fraud and abuse in health care, and to standardize record keeping, making information sharing between medical facilities and practitioners easier. The privacy rules that are part of Title II are the source of the current patient confidentiality requirements that law enforcement and security professionals need to understand.

DOCTOR-PATIENT CONFIDENTIALITY

The idea of keeping patients' information confidential has been derived from the ethical standards that doctors have promised to uphold since Roman times. This oath translates to our modern **doctor-patient confidentiality**. One of the phrases of the Hippocratic Oath, traditionally taken by doctors swearing to practice their art ethically, is "What I may see or hear in the course of treatment or even outside of the treatment in regard to the life of men, which on no account one must spread abroad, I will keep myself holding such things shameful to be spoken about."

The need for this secrecy is obvious when considered carefully. Doctors know the most intimate details of their patients' anatomy, habits, and health. If doctors could not be trusted to keep these details secret, then patients would be far less likely to seek out treatment for embarrassing or socially unacceptable ailments, either for themselves or for their family members. How much less likely would an underage person be to seek treatment for alcohol poisoning after a college party if that information would be made public? Would a parent be as willing to take their overdosed adult child to the hospital if it might make the next day's local news?

Western society expects doctors to adhere to this principle, in part because the relationship between doctors and patients is so uneven in power. The doctor knows the patient's secrets, but the patient does not know the doctor's. This confidentiality expectation is in force even after the patient stops seeing the doctor. This confidentiality is not absolute, however. Even before HIPAA was enacted, doctors could be compelled by law to report cases of deadly, contagious diseases like smallpox or tuberculosis to government authorities tasked with maintaining public health. Even though the information was no longer only between the doctor and patient, it was still only to be divulged to those with a specific need to know. There are other exceptions in force today, which will be covered later in this Module.

In the past, doctors compounded drugs themselves, kept their own records, and treated their patients in the patients' homes. Now, of course, not only are there doctors, but also an army of nurses, technicians, office staff, and administrators that oversee various parts of a patient's treatment, record maintenance, and billing, all of who adopt a codes of ethics and oaths that mirror the Hippocratic promise of confidentiality.

The more people who know a secret, the more likely it is to be inappropriately shared. Though the vast majority of people with access to this information are both ethically conscientious and well intentioned, we have all seen in the news how inducements of money could buy any major celebrity's health information from some unethical health care worker. The vast amount of paperwork generated in a modern medical facility, and the use of computer record-keeping systems of various levels of sophistication and security consciousness, guarantee that much of that leaked information is simply carelessly or thoughtlessly shared.

The Evolution of HIPAA

Though many states had laws protecting medical information, they were a patchwork of rules that were very difficult to follow when information needed to be transferred from one doctor or hospital to another across state lines. Patients could never really know how their private information was being protected.

When Title II's Administrative Simplification Rules defined how information should be collected and formatted, it was in an attempt to make health care information more efficiently shared whenever necessary. Title II also included the **Privacy Rule**, which helped to ensure that information is not misused under any circumstance. The Privacy Rule came with many provisions and requirements about protecting **protected health information** (PHI), which includes any information that concerns a patient's health status, treatments, or payments that can be linked to an individual. These provisions include:

- Requiring patient consent to release PHI, and to release only the minimum PHI that the receiver needs to achieve its purpose

- Requiring that a patient's own PHI be given to them within 30 days of the request, and to allow a patient to replace any inaccurate information

- Requiring entities with PHI to track how that information is disclosed

- Holders of PHI must have policies in place to protect that information, and must train their employees in those policies

PHI includes all information that would allow the medical record to be matched with an individual patient. Theoretically, if all PHI were scrubbed from the record, it would no longer be protected, and such cleaned records could be used for research or education. This means that, for instance, heart rhythm strips or lab results from real patients that have all of the patient's information removed could be used to teach interpretation of heart rhythm strips or lab results.

Examples of PHI include, but are not limited to:

- Names
- All geographic references smaller than a state, including:
  - street address
  - city
  - county
  - zip codes

- Telephone, cell or fax number
- Email addresses
- Social Security numbers
- Medical record numbers
- Health plan account numbers
- Other account numbers
- All elements of dates (except years), including:
  - birth date
  - admission date
  - discharge date
  - date of death
- Certificate/license numbers
- Vehicle identifiers including license plate numbers
- URLs and IP addresses
- Biometric identifiers, including fingerprints
- Full face photographic images and any comparable images

How Does HIPAA Affect Police?

Police officers have a world of restrictions on their activities that favor the rights of the individual citizens they serve. The rules of evidence, arrest, search, and seizure do not change in a hospital. Think of HIPAA restrictions as the evidence rules that medical staff members must follow, rather than as roadblocks to your investigation.

A police official can call a hospital to find if an individual is a patient there, though it is important to understand that many hospitals allow patients to opt out of the public directory. This means that a patient may be in the hospital but not show up on the computer when the directory is searched. Hospital staff members are allowed to give more information to police who arrive in person, because they can verify the identity of the officer in a way that is impossible over the telephone. The very fact that the person is a patient is PHI, but allowing that person to be on the directory makes it publicly available and no longer protected.

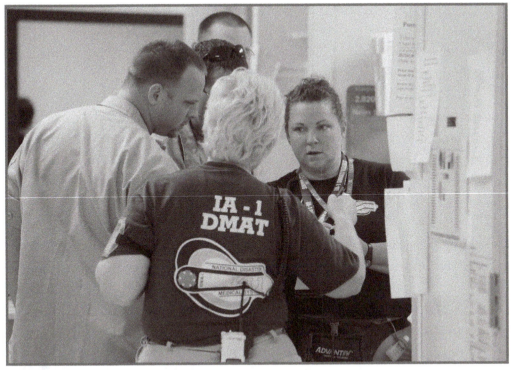

FIGURE 8.1: *The tension between law enforcement and medical personnel can be avoided if the ramifications of HIPPA are clearly understood by both agencies.*

Staff must first determine that the requester is actually a police official. Usually arriving in uniform is enough, but they are not out of line if they ask to see a department-issued picture ID card as well. The officer will have to explain what information he seeks and why, so that the hospital can give only the information required in order to protecting the patient's right to confidentiality. For example, if police are seeking a man identified by an assault victim who claims to have stabbed his attacker in self defense, the hospital may disclose that the man is a patient, and whethre or not he is being treated for knife wounds. His current treatment for alcohol abuse or pneumonia is not important to the police investigation, and would be protected information. Some information will be more protected due to its sensitivity.

Most health care systems have rules that require written requests for information about mental health, HIV testing or genetic information. These requests should be presented on proper stationary (marked with the department's seal demonstrating that the bearer is working under departmental authority) and detail the information required with brief explanations of why the information is important to the investigation.

Police Access to Patients

A police officer may need to interview a patient in relation to crimes committed outside the hospital or on hospital grounds. The patient's health and safety are the paramount concern, but officers can be allowed to interview patients when it is safe to do so.

Generally, the on-duty physician must be asked first if the patient can safely be interviewed. If the patient's care will not be negatively impacted, the patient will then be asked if he would be willing to speak to the police. A patient does not have to speak to the police any more than a person on the street does. If a patient requests to speak to police, he may do so, even if the doctor believes it would be harmful. Nonetheless, an officer should be careful to impact the care of a patient as little as possible.

Resource - Here are the rules as explained by the Department of Health and Human Services, the federal government agency responsible for enforcing HIPAA.

www.hhs.gov/hipaafaq/permitted/law/505.html

Mandatory Reporting Rules

HIPAA and other privacy rules are intended to ensure that health information is kept confidential, in order to build the necessary trust between patient and caregiver. However, these rules are not absolute. Just as protecting life takes priority over protecting property in a police officer's regular day, privacy takes a back seat to protection when the most vulnerable members of our society are at risk, or when evidence of serious crimes are uncovered medically.

Every state has laws requiring the reporting of suspected child abuse, but laws vary about reporting elder abuse or domestic violence. Police officers want to know when these crimes occur, and health care providers want to report these crimes. Unfortunately, there is confusion within the health care industry about the circumstances covered by HIPAA, which was never intended to protect or hide abuse, neglect or assault.

Child Abuse

Police officers and health care workers feel the same disgust for child abuse and abusers. The combination of righteous anger at the abuser and the utter disbelief that any adult could do such things to a child creates a team of police and health care providers who are invested in protecting abused children. The laws in every state are unambiguous when it comes to where the responsibility for reporting suspected child abuse falls.

Broadly, **child abuse** is an act or failure to act that results in, or creates an imminent risk of serious physical or emotional harm to a child. This harm is caused by a parent or caretaker who is responsible for the child's welfare. Neglect is an example of failure to act in a child's best interest that can cause risk of harm. Parental substance abuse or involvement in the manufacture, sale, or distribution of illegal drugs are other situations which also create immediate risk of harm to a child, even if such harm has not yet occurred.

Who is required to report suspected child abuse? In every state the following personnel are required to report suspected child abuse:

- All health care providers
- Mental health care providers
- Teachers and all school workers
- Social workers
- Day care providers
- All law enforcement workers

Many states go further, and require any person who suspects child abuse to report it to authorities. For instance, many reports have been made by film processors who saw photographs of what they interpreted as abusive practices, or by neighbors who saw patterns of abusive behavior. Making an allegation of child abuse is a serious matter, and should not be made without evidence. Some states require that reports be based on "reasonable suspicion," while others require the reporter to "know or suspect," which is a higher level of certainty. Police officers and health care workers are educated in this area, and should know what their local laws require.

Domestic Violence

Unlike suspected child abuse, however, there is no legal requirement for health care providers to report suspected domestic violence in most states, although many consider it an ethical requirement. PHI is not protected by HIPAA when a crime is involved, so even if state law does not require reporting, HIPAA allows for it. Many health care workers do not know this, and so they will not report domestic violence for fear of violating patient privacy rules.

Domestic violence is defined differently by each state, but police and health care workers generally get involved when the abuse involves physical or sexual assault. Though it is far more often a male abuser and a female victim, women can be abusers and men the victims. Studies show that abuse occurs in same-sex couples at about the same rate as in heterosexual couples, though it is more often overlooked in same-sex relationships.

The question of whether reporting should be mandatory is complex. Many domestic violence victim advocates believe that mandatory reporting would reduce the chances of victims seeking medical help, as it is often their abusers that take them to the emergency room. For the same reason, health care workers may be less likely to report suspicions of abuse. The practical difference between reporting child abuse versus domestic violence is that children are less able to protect themselves physically or leave an abusive situation than an abused adult. This does not imply that adult victims are somehow complicit in their abuse, as the physical and psychological barriers in place over long periods of abuse can make their ability to leave nearly as difficult.

Elder Abuse

Elder abuse is becoming a more important issue that police and health care workers face daily. Elder abuse can take many forms; in this Module, we will discuss the types of abuse that are most often seen by law enforcement or health care, which are physical assault and neglect.

Elder abuse can be very difficult to identify, which leads to underreporting. The basic definition of **elder abuse** involves an older person who has suffered deprivation, injury, or unnecessary danger through the action or (inaction) of one or more persons who bear responsibility for their care. As in the other forms of abuse we discussed, it is the trust relationship that elevates this crime above mere assault.

As in domestic violence, which is a closely related crime, state laws vary widely across the country. Elder abuse is a crime in every state, but reporting requirements are inconsistent, with some states requiring reporting by any witness, others by specified professionals, and still others encouraging, but not requiring, reporting.

R

Resource - The National Center on Elder Abuse is a department of the U.S. Administration on Aging. Established in 1988, its purpose is to educate and train both professionals and the general public about elder abuse. Their goals are to ensure the fair treatment and dignity of older Americans. For more information about training, community outreach and resources, go to:

http: //www.ncea.aoa.gov/

The arguments for and against mandatory reporting are similar to those for domestic violence. For instance, it can be very difficult to know whether an elderly person's injury was due to abuse or simply from an accidental fall. Dementia, whether diagnosed or undiagnosed, makes the victim a potentially unreliable witness. A family's desire to respect an older member's wish to live independently is not neglectful if that person is injured in a fall or stops eating for several days. Often, medical personnel, police investigators, and the possible victim must work together to determine whether a crime has been committed.

CASE STUDY

A Louisiana hospital found itself at the center of a HIPAA controversy some years ago when a nurse reported to police that she was giving care to a victim of domestic violence.

The state does not require reporting from health care givers for suspected domestic violence, but the police are required to investigate every domestic violence report they receive. When officers arrived to investigate the report, a case manager stopped them from interviewing the victim. The case manager claimed that she had spoken to the victim, who did not want to speak to the police. She further stated that HIPAA protected this information from the police investigators, and that the nurse had violated the act in reporting the suspected crime. She threatened the officers with a lawsuit, and refused to allow the officers to investigate the report. She was later arrested for interfering with law enforcement in the course of their duties, and later sued the officers for false arrest and asked for a large amount of money in damages.

The court dismissed the case. Part of the court's opinion reads: "HIPAA prohibits hospital personnel from disclosing protected health care information to third parties. It does not bar police officers from obtaining information related to a perpetrated crime directly from a patient, nor does it prohibit hospital personnel from allowing police officers access to a patient who was a victim of a crime."

If you were one of the responding officers, how would you explain the situation in order to gain voluntary compliance from the case manager? If your educational efforts failed, what other resources would be available that might hold greater weight with her?

Working With Hospital Staff

Police officers have to be able to work in any environment within their area of responsibility, and must be able to communicate with anyone they meet there. The population they serve may range the entire socioeconomic and educational spectrum, and that population's expectations from and reactions to police officers will change just as drastically. Good officers adjust to the challenge of maintaining professional relations with anyone along that continuum.

Hospitals are often difficult places for police officers to work. Officers working for specific departments at a hospital or university quickly learn the balancing act, but for those whose jobs require visits to clear prisoners for booking or for investigations, the hospital campus is somewhat alien territory. They are often small cities in themselves, with all the services necessary for operating 24 hours a day, every day of the year. The staff required to operate the campus are extremely diverse in background and education.

At a large university medical center, officers may encounter doctors and research scientists who are world-renowned experts in their fields, as well as professional administrators responsible for budgets that dwarf the budgets of some cities. There will be dozens, or even hundreds, of mid-level doctors and nurses, medical technicians of all kinds, engineers keeping all of the specialized equipment running, cooks, cleaners; there is, in fact, a small army working behind the scenes. The patients and their families and visitors add a whole second layer of complexity to the environment for an outsider like a responding officer.

Navigating the Campus

Bringing prisoners to the emergency department for **clearance** before booking, or an inmate to a scheduled medical appointment, is a relatively simple task that a new officer will be taught to do during field training. Responding to a call for an on-campus crime or investigation can be much more complicated. In these circumstances, the officer will need help from the hospital's staff, help that will be far more cheerfully given if the officer asks for it rather than demands it. Remember that hospital personnel are often very busy and that their priorities are not the same as law enforcement's priorities. For example, insisting on interviewing an emergency room doctor as an ambulance is pulling up to the doors is not only doomed to failure, but may alienate the doctor and make it less likely that doctor will find time to speak to you, even after the emergency.

The rhythm of a busy medical center is not immediately obvious to those who do not work there. Fortunately, there are many resources available on-site that can be used to find people, places, and information.

Hospital Security and Police

Officers should try to cultivate a relationship with the members of the hospital's security department. Many large university hospitals have campus police, as well as security guards, and while they are both generally very willing to help officers from outside agencies, the security guards are usually more numerous and immediately available.

Working the hospital beat is much like working a small city, and the people who do it get to know almost everyone. This means that even if the security officer does not know how to find a person or piece of information, he is very likely to know who would. Communicating with the hospital's campus security officer when conducting an investigation or doing any police business in the hospital is always a good idea. Not only is it polite to acknowledge his important responsibilities, but also remember that he is your backup should you need help. He can get to you to help much faster if he knows where you are going in the hospital.

Blood Draws

Police often want to collect blood as evidence in cases potentially involving alcohol or drugs. Blood alcohol levels are unassailable evidence in cases where driving under the influence is suspected. How do officers get this blood?

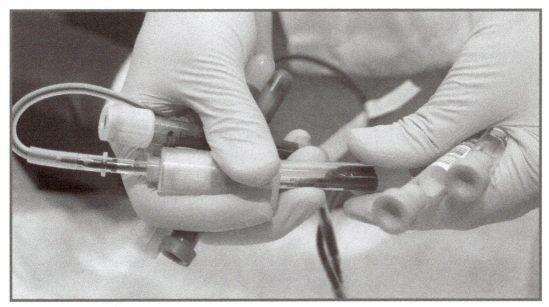

FIGURE 8.2: *There is specific protocol that law enforcement must follow when obtaining medical evidence, such as blood samples.*

Just like any other evidence, blood must be collected by technicians who are trained in specific procedures and in the handling of evidence. For that reason, police departments usually have trained technicians on-call, who can come to a hospital or stationhouse to draw blood on demand. Sometimes large, urban hospitals will have a staff member on-site who is qualified to perform this service. Using this sort of resource not only helps ensure that the sample is collected and processed in the best way for the best result, but also reduces the openings for a defense lawyer to create doubt over the test's reliability should the case go to trial.

What happens if a police technician cannot respond, or if the suspect is rushed into surgery before blood can be taken? Can medical staff take the blood sample? Is it reasonable to think that hospital staff would check blood alcohol levels before giving other medications that might interact dangerously with alcohol?

Medical staff can draw blood. Generally, the law allows doctors, nurses, phlebotomists, and EMTs to draw blood for evidentiary use, but they are usually not trained to draw samples for use as evidence. Police investigators can get access to medical records relating to blood tests performed with a court order, but this is not ideal for several reasons.

A suspect has the right to question his accusers and examine evidence. This means that the defense could summon every person who ever handled the sample to testify, from the nurse who drew the blood to the lab techs who processed it, to the clerk who input the information into the computer records, to verify that the blood was not tampered with or mislabeled. All of those employees' supervisors could be called to testify that the staff had been trained in and properly followed all written procedures. The procedures themselves would be scrutinized to verify that they would not cause a false result, and that they conformed to the current standards and best practices. An otherwise simple case of alcohol or drug intoxication could be drawn out over weeks.

There are also concerns that the results of blood alcohol levels in the hospital, which usually tests serum or plasma, would be different than the approved test, which uses **whole blood**, or blood before it is centrifuged to separate it into its solid and liquid parts. Blood that is drawn after a suspect has received intravenous fluids is also suspect, and can actually read falsely high as the fluid brings alcohol out of the tissues and into the bloodstream faster than would naturally occur. Some states do not allow hospital-run blood samples to be used in court because of these concerns.

When a trained police technician draws the blood, most of those doubts are removed. Specifically approved techniques and equipment are used that have already been accepted as valid by the courts. The chain of custody is easier to follow, as the tech takes the blood, and either gives it to the officer for forwarding to the lab with any other evidence or takes it himself.

Asking the hospital staff to draw blood for evidence is not a good practice unless there is a policy in place that allows it and answers the above concerns. Privacy and HIPAA concerns will sometimes be voiced by staff that mean well but are not fully versed in the law, but education is the answer, not the argument. The blood test is simply one piece of evidence among many. It is important, but it is not always required to prosecute the case.

Suspect Identification

Before a suspect can be prosecuted, police have to find out who the suspect is. This very simple concept drives much of the investigation of any serious crime, as once an individual is identified as likely to have committed the crime, the tools that the investigators can use increase dramatically. On TV, crimes are solved when the suspect is identified through fingerprints, high-tech DNA testing, or clever ploys in which the criminal is tricked into confessing guilt. While those do play a role in real life, the majority of suspects are identified through witness or victim descriptions.

Interviewing Tips

Descriptions gained from interviews can be used to narrow the list of possible suspects, and to create suspect sketches or lineups that are defensible in court. Unless the officer uses good interviewing techniques to pull useful information from a witness or victim, investigators may not have enough information to work with, or may rule out the actual criminal because he doesn't match the description.

Interviewing witnesses and victims is the first step in suspect identification, and it is not an easy skill to develop without practice. During and after training, you will work with officers who are able to get the maximum amount of correct information out of witnesses. They should become your role models and mentors as you learn the necessary interviewing skills.

Witnesses who are comfortable are generally able to provide the best information. It is important to build rapport with the subject so that he believes that his statements are relevant. Starting the interview conversationally, even with a simple "how are you?" can help the subject to relax, and also allows the interviewer to get a feeling for how the subject communicates. It also helps the interviewer notice issues such as drunkenness or confusion that might make the statements less reliable. Getting the statement as soon as possible after the event is important. Even the most cooperative witness can become an unreliable reporter if her memory is allowed to fade. Active listening is another tactic for demonstrating to the witness that her statement is being carefully considered.

Active listening involves periodically restating the witness's statement back to him or her in the interviewer's own words, which helps to ensure that her report is being clearly understood, as well as showing the witness that her report is valued.

Witnesses should be separated before interviewing, and should always be interviewed separately. Witnesses should not hear each other's accounts, in order to protect the independence of their memories. A less secure witness may be tempted to change his report to match the story of another witness who seems very certain, because the subject does not trust his own memory. Invariably, the accounts will differ somewhat from witness to witness, depending on the circumstances, even when witnesses are being truthful.

Ask witnesses open-ended questions, which do not allow yes or no answers, but rather are more detailed descriptions and recollections. For each topic, the interviewer should start with open-ended questions, and then elicit details using closed-ended questions as needed.

FIGURE 8.3: *Witness statements frequently lead to suspect identification.*

Witnesses will sometimes have trouble providing descriptions; the interviewer can request more detail, but must be careful not to lead the witness' memories. If the suspect is described as tall, but the witness is unsure how tall, the height can often be narrowed by asking whether the suspect was taller or shorter than a person nearby. Having someone of known height to compare his/her memory against is often helpful.

Show-Ups and Lineups

We've all seen lineups on TV shows and movies, but show-ups are much more common in real police work. A **show-up** is usually done very shortly after a crime has occurred. If officers find a suspect shortly after the crime is committed, they may bring the suspect back to the scene, or take the witness to where the suspect is held, so that the witness can identify (or not identify) the suspect.

A show–up should only be used if the witness has already provided a good description of the suspect. If the witness only says, "I didn't see him well. It was too dark," then the concern would be that simply seeing someone in custody would encourage the witness to identify that person as the suspect. For the same reason, it should be conducted shortly after the crime, when the witness's memory is still sharp.

Police must have reasonable suspicion to detain a suspect for a show-up. **Reasonable suspicion** is a lower level of certainty than probable cause, and can be reached by an officer who has heard a basic description of the suspect over the radio. This is one reason that suspect descriptions should be broadcast to other units as soon as possible after the crime has occurred.

Though lineups as portrayed in the media seem like a simple procedure, they must be crafted very carefully in order to be used as evidence. Frequently, lineups can be completed using photographs. Whether live or photographic, the members of the lineup must be physically similar, while matching the witness's description. If the suspect was described as a 5' tall blonde woman, a lineup with four brunettes taller than 5'8" and one 5' blonde would not be valid. Further, when photographs are used for a lineup, the photos must all be the same size and of the same quality. Mixing black and white with color, or booking style mug shots with full body photos, would potentially be too suggestive to survive court review. A good practice is to create two or more lineups that include the suspect to see if the witness identifies the same one each time. With visible tattoos and piercings becoming ever more popular, each member of the lineup would be required to have similar markings, which can be very difficult to create.

Police departments now have many booking photos available electronically, and software is available that can create photo lineups from those photo databanks. Human operators must still check the output to ensure that the lineups are appropriately populated. Once the lineup is accepted, the software also automates the process for saving the lineup for later court use.

Live lineups create a series of problems, so they are used much less often. Finding six or eight people of even broadly similar appearance can be difficult, but they also must be demonstrating similar behavior and demeanor. An uncooperative suspect can invalidate the whole lineup by acting belligerent or in a bizarre fashion.

Suspect Sketches

The human memory is notoriously unreliable. In order to freeze a witness's memory of a suspect's appearance, **sketches** have long been made based on their descriptions. The quality of these sketches has varied widely, depending on the accuracy of the artist and the quality of the witness's description. Once the sketch is made, copies can be distributed to officers and to the general public, or even shown on TV with the hope that someone will see it and identify the individual.

FIGURE 8.4: *If correct information is supplied, suspect sketches can be a helpful tool in the identification process.*

Sketch Artists

Drawing a recognizable face from witness statements is not easy. The person sketching has to be both a technically capable artist, as well as a master interviewer, and neither of these skills is easy to learn. **Forensic artists**, as police sketch artists are now called, are often able to do more than simply reproduce a face from a description. They pursue training in anatomy, odontology (the structure and growth of teeth), psychology, and even age progression, which is the practice of producing a picture of what a person looks like after a long period of time.

The artist's training in police work and psychology also makes these people valuable resources during the investigation. Not every witness is cooperative, and some may attempt to dupe the artist into making a sketch that is inaccurate. The length of time that the artist must spend with the witness to create a sketch, and the depth of the interviewing required, can often uncover portions of a witness's memory that other interviewers missed, or unearth evidence that the witness is being less than truthful.

Computerized Drawings and Composites

The difficulty of finding people with all the necessary skills and knowledge to become forensic sketch artists, along with the explosion in the power of affordable computers, has spurred efforts to create products that allow almost any officer to create images of suspects.

The earliest efforts involved facial features and hairstyles printed on transparent sheets, which could be stacked to produce a composite image. A **composite image** is one made when many parts are added together. A witness would be interviewed and then shown a composite image, which he could then critique. The interviewer then adjusted each portion of the image with different details until the witness was satisfied that it represented the person he remembered. This is a time consuming process, as each face might have a dozen features, and each feature could have several dozen options to choose from. These composite images were generally flat-looking pictures, made of black lines on a white background, with little to no shading.

As relatively inexpensive desktop computers became more powerful, image manipulation software became available that even small law enforcement departments could afford to purchase and utilize. The general concept is the same as the older manual composite kits, but the features in each face can be manipulated more subtly and with an almost infinite progression of changes. Enormous databases of images that have already been produced are available, and can give a starting point for a new image, which might be easier to manipulate than a bare page. The output of these computerized composite programs can be much more lifelike than the manual composite kits provided, with the best producing photo-realistic images of the suspect.

Computerized composite sketches are efficient and available for use by officers with very little training, but if used by an officer who is not skillful at interviewing witnesses, the results may be ineffective. A bad sketch is worse than none at all, as it can create doubt in a jury if the sketch is too unlike the suspect standing in the courtroom.

EXAMPLE: The UNABOM case was one of the FBI's most extensive investigations. The UNABOM case name originally stood for UNiversity and Airline BOMber, and the media dubbed the perpetrator Unabomber. Over the course of almost 20 years, the suspect sent 16 bombs via the mail, killing three people and injuring 23 others.

The famous composite sketch made of the Unabomber, commissioned by the FBI and drawn by artist Jeanne Boylan, is used as evidence of both the value and failure of forensic sketches. Boylan's sketch was shown throughout the country for years, raising public awareness of the crimes, but when Ted Kaczynski was finally arrested, many noticed that the drawing resembled him very little. The supposed lack of resemblance fuels conspiracy theories linking him to the CIA and alleged mind control experiments to this day.

Though the sketch was not instrumental in identifying the Unabomber, who was eventually captured after family members recognized his writing style in his newspaper-published manifesto, its widespread distribution almost certainly reduced Kaczynski's ability to safely travel. In 1985, the Unabomber sent four bombs, and one in 1987 before the sketch was shown. After the sketch's release in 1987, there were no bombs sent for almost five years.

So why does the sketch look so little like Kaczynski's booking picture? The sketch shows a man wearing a hooded sweatshirt and very large sunglasses; much of his face is not visible. The witness saw only that much, and only for a short time. It should also be realized that nine years passed between the sketch's release and the arrest, and during that time Kaczynski lived in a wilderness shack without power or water. His booking picture shows a man who looks far older than his 53 years.

Summary

Police officers have frequent interactions with the health care system. The rules that medical professionals abide by are as important to them as law enforcement policies are to officers. HIPAA is one such important law, though many health care workers do not fully understand it. The Privacy Rule portion of HIPAA is intended to ensure that private health care information remains private, but it was never intended to get in the way of a criminal investigation.

The law requires certain crimes to be reported by medical staff, and since this can change by state, it is important to be sure what your state's laws require. The education of medical staff members who misunderstand the law should be a priority for any officer who spends much time in the local hospitals.

The people who work in health care have different priorities than police officers, but share a similar desire to serve their communities and solve problems. This similarity should be a starting point in the relationship between the hospital and law enforcement. A typical hospital has hundreds, or even thousands, of workers at all levels, many of who can be asked for different levels of assistance. The security department is a great resource for visiting officers, and a close working relationship is also an officer safety benefit.

Skill in interviewing witnesses and victims of crimes is an important tool for officers to develop. Whether used to get a description for arranging a lineup, or for creating a composite sketch, the essential first step is a thorough interview completed as soon as possible after the event.

Discussion Questions

1. Do the HIPAA restrictions on information disclosure seem appropriate to you? Why or why not?

2. What are your thoughts about mandatory reporting of suspected domestic violence or elder care?

3. Have you seen or heard any examples of very good or very ineffective interview methods? What might some differences in approach be if interviewing an older physician, as compared to interviewing a younger hospital housekeeper?

4. What techniques would you use to calm a crime victim still in shock after an assault in order to get a suspect description as soon as possible?

5. One reason that sketch artists are becoming rarer is that the increasing number of cameras in the cities often provides photographs of suspects. Where are these cameras located in your city or town? Can you count on that option where you live?

Key Terms

Chain of custody — The record showing that evidence was properly maintained and protected from tampering from collection until presentation in court.

Child abuse — An act or failure to act that results in, or creates an imminent risk of, serious harm, physical or emotional, to a child by a parent or caretaker who is responsible for the child's welfare.

Clearance — The medical process that verifies a prisoner is medically safe to be booked into jail. Often required when a prisoner has been using alcohol or drugs, or when force is needed to accomplish the arrest.

Composite image — A single image created through the overlay of several discreet features.

Doctor-patient confidentiality — The ethical requirement for physicians to protect their patients' private health information.

Domestic violence — A pattern of behavior used to establish power and control over an intimate partner through fear and intimidation, often including the threat or use of violence.

Elder abuse — Causing an elderly person deprivation, injury, or unnecessary danger through the action or inaction of one or more persons who bear responsibility for that person's care.

Forensic artists — Artists who combine drawing skill with scientific knowledge to create pictures of suspects or others from witness descriptions or forensic evidence.

The Health Insurance Portability and Accountability Act (HIPAA) — The Health Insurance Portability and Accountability Act, which made provision for workers to keep their health insurance when changing jobs, and also increased regulation for record keeping and privacy standards.

Lineup — A live or photographic presentation where a witness is asked to identify a suspect.

Privacy Rule — The part of HIPAA relating to patient health information protection.

Protected health information (PHI) — The information maintained by health care organizations that allows an individual to be identified.

Reasonable suspicion — A belief based on specific facts that an individual was involved in a crime.

Show-up — Usually held shortly after a crime is witnessed where the suspect is shown to the witness for identification in the field.

Sketch — A drawing based on a witness's description and intended for use in suspect identification or for other evidentiary reasons.

Whole blood — Blood before it is centrifuged to separate it into its solid and liquid parts.

MODULE 9
Applied Skills: Use of Force

Key Module Concepts:

- Ethical and legal considerations in the use of force

- Appropriate tactical communication and defensive tactics when working with the public

- Circumstances that may justify use of deadly force

- Escalation and de-escalation of force

- Proper documentation for use of force encounters

Introduction

Everyone has the right to defend himself, as well as innocent third parties, through the use of reasonable force. Officers have additional authority to use force to gain compliance and control when making arrests. Using force carries great personal and professional liability.

Enforcing laws and protecting the public can often be accomplished with conversational skills, while at other times, officers may be required to respond with physical force, including **lethal force**. Between these responses lie a wide range of alternative options and decision points. The men and women who enforce the law and provide security are given authority to deal with crime and violence by use of what is called *reasonable force*.

Everyone who works in the criminal justice field should be fully aware of the tactics, procedures, and liability involved in the use of force. They must be able to recognize and explain use of force events to those who are not professionals in the field, and to recognize any incident of abuse that may be observed. It is critical to be able to rationally and logically understand the reasons for use of force, and to use force only when necessary.

In this Module, we will discuss some of the key issues in identifying when to use force, what force is appropriate, the documentation of the use of force, and the ramifications of using force.

Ask Yourself

- *What are some considerations for officers when using force options?*

- *Other than weapons, what other tools are essential for officers?*

- *What ramifications could occur when deadly force is used?*

- *How can emotions obscure the officer's performance?*

Force Decision Stakeholders

Law enforcement officers should be aware that there are a number of individuals, entities, and other stakeholders involved in every use of force decision. When taking action in a use of force encounter, officers represent:

- Themselves
- Other officers
- The agency's executive staff (for example, chief or sheriff)
- Government (elected officials overseeing the agency)
- Public interests

The officers involved in a use of force case are likely to be named as defendants if a lawsuit is filed, along with the agency heads and government officials. If the lawsuit is lost and damages are assessed, the taxpayers will foot the bill.

Financial exposure aside, the stakeholders have a shared interest in high-quality, reasonable, and fair law enforcement.

Rules Governing the Use of Force

The legal use of force by law enforcement is not intended for punishing criminals, which is not the job or responsibility of a police officer. The officer's objective is to ultimately gain or maintain control of subjects being arrested or detained.

Using **control** to apprehend a suspect means using only the force necessary to make an arrest or to gain compliance. Since law enforcement personnel have the authority to make arrests and promote safety, it is the utmost importance that they develop skills and knowledge to do so with reasonable force.

Reasonable force is defined as what force an officer would use based on the knowledge of the moment when the force is used, rather than 20/20 hindsight. The legal term reasonable force was established in 1989, in the case of **Graham v. Connor**, when the Supreme Court determined that the defendant's Fourth Amendment right to unreasonable seizure had been violated.

Graham v. Connor can be considered a good starting point case for understanding the meaning of the term "reasonable use of force." In this case, DeThorne Graham was driven by a friend, Berry, to a convenience store in order to buy some orange juice. Graham was experiencing a reaction due to diabetes and was seeking sugar to abate the reaction. When Graham entered the store he saw a long line at the counter, so he quickly left without waiting to buy the juice.

Officer Connor, who was not aware and had no reasonable way of knowing about Graham's situation, observed Graham hastily entering and exiting the convenience store. This unusual behavior captured his attention, and he conducted an investigatory stop of the car in which Graham left the scene. During his investigation, Connor demonstrated unusual behavior by running around the police car twice and then passing out in front of it. The officer concluded that Graham was possibly intoxicated and other officers came to the scene.

In the Supreme Court decision, the justices noted that:

> *Respondent backup police officers arrived on the scene, handcuffed Graham, and ignored or rebuffed attempts to explain and treat Graham's condition. During the encounter, Graham sustained multiple injuries...One of the officers rolled Graham over on the sidewalk and cuffed his hands tightly behind his back, ignoring Berry's pleas to get him some sugar. Another officer said, "I've seen a lot of people with sugar diabetes that never acted like this...." Several officers then lifted Graham up from behind,*

carried him over to Berry's car, and placed him face down on its hood. Regaining consciousness, Graham asked the officers to check in his wallet for a diabetic decal that he carried. In response, one of the officers told him to "shut up" and shoved his face down against the hood of the car...Four officers grabbed Graham and threw him headfirst into the police car. A friend of Graham's brought some orange juice to the car, but the officers refused to let him have it. Finally, Officer Connor received a report that Graham had done nothing wrong at the convenience store, and the officers drove him home and released him.

During this encounter, Graham sustained multiple injuries, including a broken foot, cuts on his wrists, a bruised forehead, and an injured shoulder.

This case set a standard for evaluating use of force under the Fourth Amendment (search and seizure), rather than the standards of the Eighth Amendment (cruel and unusual punishment). That means that a standard of "reasonableness" is used, as opposed to a standard that considers the officer's state of mind and requires malicious intent. The court noted in its opinion that an officer's ill intentions will not make a Fourth Amendment violation out of an objectively reasonable use of force; nor will an officer's good intentions make an objectively unreasonable use of force Constitutional.

Objective Reasonableness

To determine the **objective reasonableness** for any use of force, the Court established a standard for police. The ruling declared that the events must be "fact specific." The classifications of reasonableness to a particular use of force are the following:

• Judged from the perspective of a officer

• Examined through the eyes of an officer at the scene where the force was used, and not the 20/20 vision of hindsight

- Based on the circumstances the officer confronted without any underlying intent and/or motivation

- Based on a proper reaction as per training under the current established law

The Court has also noted other factors for measuring reasonableness. These factors include, but are not limited to severity of the crime; subject's attempt to avoid detention by fleeing; nature and extent of risk created by the subject; and degree to which the subject resists arrest or custody.

Agency Policies

Agency policies regarding use of force are typically based on the current case law and relevant statutes regarding force. It is common for the agency policy to be even more restrictive than the law. Although the laws are fairly universal, the limitations on use of force may differ from one jurisdiction to another, based on the individual agency policies. Such policies are designed to be more restrictive than the law, in order to minimize the risk of liability.

Methods Of Control And Cooperation

The decision process in the use of force is fairly straightforward from a theoretical point of view. The force must be sufficient to gain control and compliance, yet not excessive. But how do you determine what is reasonable, what is enough, and what is too much? Every situation that an officer faces will be different; hence, there are no universal answers.

The officer must understand the **force options** available to him and balance them with the levels of resistance or non-compliance demonstrated by the suspect. The officer also must have a thorough understanding of the legal and reasonable application of the particular defensive tools utilized during a lawful use of force. Obtaining this knowledge takes a mixture of training, practice, and experience.

In the middle of a dangerous situation, an officer instinctively reverts to skills learned during academy training. Therefore, the quality of an officer's tactical response depends on how frequently and effectively the officer has practiced the skills. The effective use of communication and defensive skills are the most important components of such confrontations.

The elements of force that are available to an officer begin with the commanding presence of a uniformed officer and a high level of verbal communication skills. The elements escalate to tactics such as, control holds, strikes, chemical agents, and firearms.

Even with a wide range of weapons, skills, and tactics, the outcome of events can be unpredictable and the consequences unintended. For example, in October 2010, Australian officers responded to a sexual assault call when they encountered Le Ba Thinh wielding two large knives, each measuring almost a foot long. As they tried to arrest Thinh, who they believed to be intoxicated, he charged at the officers with the weapons. A constable ordered him to stop. When the suspect refused to stop, the officer fired a stun gun at close range, stopping the suspect's charge. Although stun guns are considered to be a tool of less than lethal force, the man later died in the hospital.

New South Wales Police Commissioner Andrew Scipione defended the officers' actions, stating if the constable had not fired the stun gun, the confrontation would likely have resulted in severe injuries or deaths to others.

Although the situation would have probably justified the use of a firearm, having additional options that are less lethal provide some opportunity to reduce loss of life in police–suspect confrontations.

Effective Communication

Law enforcement is the embodiment of legal authority. Officers must convey to their lawful authority to a suspect in order to gain compliance. This authority is communicated through appearance, verbal communication (words), and non-verbal communication (actions).

Uniform Presence

Appearance can be a form of communication and control. In the police academy, officers are subjected to daily uniform inspections in which the supervisors provide very detailed and specific criticism about an officer's appearance. The purpose of this exercise is to provide the officer with the ability to project a commanding presence when he or she meets the public. Think about who would instill more confidence in the public when he or she arrives at a scene: an out-of shape officer wearing a wrinkled uniform with stains, or a well-groomed officer with sharp creases in the uniform and highly polished leather gear? The mere appearance of a neat, professional officer instills confidence and cooperation in the public. .

FIGURE 9.1: *An officer's uniform and general appearance contributes to his air of authority.*

An officer must also appear to be objective and impartial in all encounters. Even if one of the parties involved in a police matter has a personal friendship with the person behind the badge, the officer represents the public's interests, not the individual in the uniform. The uniform provides the individual with a psychological separation between his personal and professional life.

Article	Maintenance	Advantages
Uniform	• Proper fit • Clean, neat	• Easily recognizable • Commands presence
Gear	• Regular inspection • Good condition	• Confidence increased with available physical force
Firearm	• Serviced by trained armorer, when needed	• Confidence increased with available deadly force
Armor	• Proper fit	• Enhanced survivability
Personal Appearance	• Well groomed, no visible tattoos, alert and engaged	• Projects authority and professionalism
Vehicle	• Clean and polished, no visible damage	• Arrival at the scene in a clean, well-maintained vehicle is an element of command and authority
Shoes / Boots	• Highly polished and maintained, high quality	• Comfort and balance, professional appearance

FIGURE 9.2: *The advantages to proper uniform maintenance.*

Body Language and Verbal Communication

Weapons and uniforms command respect and project authority, but one of the most effective skills police have is effective verbal communication. Tone and word choice help an officer portray a commanding presence to the suspect(s). A strong and well-structured verbal warning, or an understanding and empathetic approach, may be all that is needed to avoid a confrontation where use of force is required. The officer must have a diverse set of verbal and body language tools to respond to all potential situations and be able to express a range of responses from actively listening to authoritarian command.

Most of what is communicated between two parties is conveyed with facial expressions and body language. Only a small percent of communications is based on the actual words used in the conversation. However, one insensitive word or poor turn of phrase can destroy any positive communication experience.

Effective verbal communication requires that an officer can quickly assess what is needed to resolve a situation and determine how to get all the parties involved to reach that conclusion. Since the initial approach, like a first impression, is the central factor that determines how others perceive the tone of everything one does, the officer's attitude and demeanor always precede his or her own words.

Additionally, the radio provides a certain level of command at a situation. The ability of the officer to immediately summon reinforcements, including SWAT teams, helicopters, and jail vans, is a powerful deterrent to resistance. A suspect who overhears a calm request for additional units to respond to your situation may reconsider any plans for resistance.

In an ideal world, the goal of the officer is to achieve compliance and cooperation from the public without relying on physical force. Effective communication is one of the most basic and easiest force options a peace officer can use.

Defense Equipment

Before we address when to use specialized tools of control, we will identify some of the equipment and techniques available to patrol officers.

A suspect's actions will determine the amount of force used, since force is always used in response to a situation. The force options run the gamut from arrival at the scene in a fully equipped patrol car with emblems, verbal commands, physical force, less than lethal or intermediate weapons, and finally to deadly force.

The weapons at the officer's disposal include personal weapons, intermediate weapons, and deadly weapons.

Personal Weapons

Officers learn techniques that utilize only the physical body rather than weapons, including the following:

Gestures: Directing with firm verbal commands and pointing or placing a palm up represents a very basic level of personal control

Restraint and control holds: Officers learn wristlocks, arm bars, and what the public generally recognizes as types of judo or wrestling moves

Personal weapons: Fist and open-hand strikes, kicks, and elbow and knee strikes can be used in highly aggressive defensive situations

Pressure point controls: By applying pressure to nerve groups, the officer can "stun" limbs and gain compliance

Carotid artery restraint: Often considered by policy as next to deadly force, the so-called "sleeper hold" is often used to render violent suspects unconscious

Intermediate Weapons

Intermediate weapons are the tools often found on an officer's duty belt, and they include the following:

Impact weapons: The police baton comes in many configurations, ranging from the traditional nightstick and the expandable baton to the side handle baton. These tools can be used for delivering powerful strikes or control holds. The impact weapon can become a lethal force tool when striking certain vital areas of the human body, such as the head or throat.

Chemical agents: Pepper spray and tear gas can quickly be deployed to disable an aggressive suspect rapidly

Electronic devices: Devices such as stun guns and Tasers can give a suspect a non-lethal, but incapacitating shock, which disrupts nerve centers without electrocuting the subject

FIGURE 9.3: *Deadly weapons should be deployed only when other methods are inappropriate or ineffective for the situation.*

Deadly Weapons

Although any technique can result in a fatality under specific circumstances, the firearm's purpose is to stop the suspect when other means have failed or are obviously inappropriate.

Firearms include the following:

Handgun: The handgun comes in a variety of forms and is carried on the officer's gun belt. Although handguns have an effective range of well over 100 yards, most gunfights occur within a range of five yards. The handgun is considered a close-range weapon.

Shotgun: The police shotgun is a deadly and powerful weapon for close and intermediate range combat. It fires a projectile of buckshot (small pellets) or a large slug.

Rifle: The rifle is an intermediate-range to long-range weapon. It is often used by SWAT teams or in patrol for long-range combat or precision shooting.

When engaging someone in a situation, a peace officer continuously evaluates and reevaluates the suspect's actions and the changing circumstances to make sure the appropriate force is being applied. To evaluate the resistance and conditions involved in use of force situations and to respond appropriately, officers learn how to use a force continuum to make their decisions.

Force Continuums

It is the subject's responsibility to submit to a lawful arrest; however, he or she will not always comply. It is the degree of resistance that determines which force option may be used by a police official. There are a number of scales and outlines, called continuums, that are utilized in developing and analyzing law enforcement policy.

In evaluating the use of force, experts consider several things, including:

- Subject action
- Officer response
- Conditions
- Escalation and de-escalation

In a use of force situation, the subject's actions are dynamic and changing unpredictably, as are the conditions surrounding the incident. Additionally, officers must use a level of force that is typically one level above the level of resistance they are facing, because they are not expected to provide an even matchup for a suspect. The changing levels on the officer's part may not always be exact and immediate. Unlike a professional boxing event, there is no referee, and the suspects are not following any particular rules or policies.

An officer also does not have to begin a confrontation with a verbal command; if lesser means do not make sense, the officer can launch a response with the appropriate level of force. For example, if an officer walks into a bank robbery with shots being fired, the officer does not need to try control holds, punches, kicks, and chemical agents before returning fire. The officer escalates immediately to the appropriate level required to deal with the threat. In this example, the appropriate response would probably be a verbal command to surrender, followed by the immediate use of a firearm.

The following chart provides a basic guideline for a force continuum.

Description of Subject's Actions	Possible Force Option
Cooperative; no resistance	• Mere professional attire • Nonverbal procedures • Verbal requests
Passive non-compliance; no physical form of resistance presented, yet unresponsive to verbal commands (for example, not fighting but not cooperating)	• Officer's strength • Control holds and techniques to direct or prevent movement
Active resistance; physical resistance to stop officer's control	• Intermediate weapons • Personal weapons (self-defense)
Life-threatening; a scenario likely resulting in serious injury or possible death	• Defensive action for self or others • Firearms or other weapons

There are a broad range of tools and techniques used by law enforcement in response to non-compliance. As a reminder, constant reevaluation of a situation is required for public safety, because conditions can change at a moment's notice. A compliant suspect may turn hostile, or a seemingly cooperative captured felon could attempt a violent escape.

Other factors or conditions include, but are not limited to:
• Age of the suspect vs. age of the officer
• Physical condition of suspect vs. condition of officer
• Number of suspects vs. number of officers
• Time of day (or night)
• Location

- Knowledge of suspect's criminal history
- Available backup for both the suspect and officer
- Whether the suspect is under the influence of a drug or intoxicated

An additional factor in evaluating a use of force incident is whether or not the use of force escalated and de-escalated. Usually in a confrontation, the resistance is not constant. The response should also scale up or down accordingly.

The officer needs to be cognizant of all of these factors to establish a reasonable level of force, and must write a detailed report that will be used to determine if the actions taken by the officer were consistent with the reasonable officer standard.

A common misconception in the use of force is the concept of "fairness." The police want to be even-handed and reasonable, but they are expected to win. If it takes three officers to subdue one combative individual without hurting him, then that is a reasonable response, although unfair in the traditional sense. It is better to have several officers wrestle the suspect to the ground rather than to knock the person unconscious with a blow to the head.

Considerations Regarding Deadly Force

Deadly force is force that creates a significant risk of inflicting death or very serious physical injury. The decision to use deadly force is one of the most stressful decisions an officer can make. It takes into account the value of human life, and should only be used when other means of control are unreasonable or have been exhausted. According to the law, fear alone is not a reasonable justification of deadly force, unless the fear is based on a reasonable belief that the officer's life or the life of an innocent third party is in immediate jeopardy.

In order to understand the aspects of the use of deadly force, police officers need to become familiar with the following terms:

Term	Definition
Serious bodily harm or injury	Severe impairment of health that includes loss of consciousness, fatal wounds, fractured bones, and internal damage
Reasonable necessity	A delayed capture would otherwise create significant danger to officers or others, possibly ensuing with serious injury or death
Imminent danger	Considerable threat that will realistically, though not always immediately, result in endangering lives

In 1984, the U.S. Supreme Court made a monumental decision to protect unarmed suspects from the use of deadly force. Ten years before, an officer, responding to a burglary call, shot 15-year-old Edward Garner in the back of the head as he fled the scene by climbing over a chain link fence. Evidence from the burglary was found on the suspect's body, but the officer was reasonably sure the suspect was not armed. According to Tennessee law, the act was legal, relying on the "fleeing felon" standard. Garner, who was unarmed, died at the hospital. His father sued. In the decision **Tennessee v. Garner**, the Court declared that

> *The use of deadly force to prevent the escape of all felony suspects, whatever the circumstances, is Constitutionally unreasonable... Where the suspect poses no immediate threat to the officer and no threat to others, the harm resulting from failing to apprehend him does not justify the use of deadly force to do so.*

Based on this decision, the law changed to restrict officers' use of deadly force in the apprehension of felons. Use of force is now limited to situations where the officer has probable cause to think that the suspect poses a significant threat of death or serious injury to the officer or others if not immediately apprehended.

When Homicide Is Justifiable

While criminal homicide is defined as the unlawful killing of a human being by another human being, under certain circumstances, a police officer's actions are deemed as **justifiable homicide**. The chart below covers such situations.

Circumstance	Reasoning
Court has determined capital punishment for a felon, thus the officer would be committing legal execution	Court order to carry out death sentence
In the midst of self defense against a perpetrator, an officer accidentally shoots and kills a bystander	Acting in the course of duty
Retaking a felon after being rescued or attempted escape	Only applies to those deemed as a threat; a fleeing felon alone is not just cause
A felon who resists arrest to the point where deadly force is reasonable	When a life is threatened or the subject could not be apprehended by other means

The determination of a justifiable homicide is not always as clear as the general guidelines used in the table. Officers will likely face the scrutiny of the courts, the agency's internal affairs division, and the press anytime lethal force is used and a human life is lost.

Deadly force encounters are rare, but like most encounters are based on decisions that must be made quickly. Split-second decisions are part of the police officer's job description. The skill to make these decisions can be developed over time through experience, and by taking into consideration the totality of circumstances, rather than allowing anger, bigotry, or fear contribute to the decision-making process.

Mitigating the impact of emotional factors involved in making a use of force decision also comes with time and experience.

Emotional Aspects

In a use of force situation, the officer will be bombarded with emotional, as well as physiological, responses. In fact, the two most powerful and natural sensations a peace officer may experience are fear and anger, so officers must demonstrate remarkable self-control.

Self-control is the act of maintaining emotional composure when making judgments and decisions, without letting certain feelings and emotions hinder performance. Self-control is a product of the effort to develop confidence and is deeply rooted in training, practice and experience. Over time, decision-making processes will improve and reaction time will decrease.

When an officer uses force, there are several factors that can influence actions and the outcome of the event. A negative attitude, prejudice, insensitivity, and arrogance can each create negative emotional and physical responses to stressful situations.

Emotional responses that are not deliberate, coupled with fear, panic, or anger can result in increased hesitation, verbal abuse, and inappropriate violence.

Facing Fear

Fear is a normal emotional response to a perceived threat; this does not become a problem until it interferes with operational judgment. While fear is unpleasant, it is sometimes normal and necessary. As Mark Twain once said, "Courage is not the absence of fear. It is acting in spite of it."

There are two types of fear: reasonable and unreasonable. **Reasonable fear** results from a legitimate threat. It can be from the sight of a subject's weapon, sudden or erratic movement, or witnessing a person in danger. **Unreasonable fear**, which may be subconscious, results from thoughts generated with no direct correlation to facts and circumstances. Recalling past traumas or dwelling on uncertainty about one's expertise can cause irrational fear. For example, a person who has a fear of snakes and has been told there are snakes in the area may overreact to the sight of a stick in the grass that looks like a snake.

One of the advantages in academy training is the concept of being desensitized to fear. By experiencing academy-controlled practice situations, officers are more rationally aware of what to expect when they have an experience in the field. For example, if a person has a fear of testifying in court, and he has to testify in mock trials in the academy, the real experience will not be so shocking or emotionally traumatic.

Additionally, the adrenaline rush experienced in high-stress situations tends to cause people to rely on their training, and the emotional response will occur after the fact.

Another technique for facing fear is the "What if" game. Mentally rehearse what situations you feel you may have to confront. For example, as you drive down the street, imagine what you would do if you saw an armed suspect coming out of a bank. Think about your options and imagine realistic positive outcomes based on your training and tactics.

- Evaluate the situation
- Determine what must be done
- Understand that the danger itself is not the true focus
- Use an internal survival phrase that controls vulnerable feelings

Internal survival phrases are also an effective technique. Tell yourself to be calm, and reiterate that you are in control of this situation. Develop a phrase that can help you snap out of any tendency to panic or be overcome by fear. Have a positive mental outlook and remember that you are a trained professional.

Managing Anger

Anger is also a normal emotion to feel when thrust into a threatening environment. As with fear, anger does not become a problem until it is deemed out of control or inappropriate. Learning how to use controlled rage positively in the line of fire can promote the mental endurance needed to win in a confrontation. When properly channeled, police have the opportunity to transform the adrenaline dump that comes with fear and anger into assertiveness.

Two types of conditions that motivate anger are labeled universal and personal. Universal examples are being attacked, shot, or agitated by a suspect. Personal examples might involve private grudges or discrimination. As with fear, you also need to prepare for situations dealing with anger by using a combination of training and mental rehearsals.

The people a society depends on for protection from criminal aggressors should never become the aggressors themselves, but sadly, it happens from time to time. **Police brutality** is a term used to describe any excessive, unnecessary use of force — physical or verbal — used by law enforcement to members of the public.

The National Police Misconduct Statistics and Reporting Project (NPMSRP) collected media and police reports between April 2009 through September 2009 concerning misconduct. Within those months, 2,854 law enforcement officers allegedly engaged in some form of misconduct. In short, roughly 14.7 incidents are reported each day on average, or a report of misconduct every 98 minutes.

There are approximately 800,000 local, state, and federal law enforcement officers in the country having multiple citizen contacts per day. These statistics may not be as bad as they sound; however, that doesn't excuse any misconduct.

Liability

There is a tremendous demand upon law enforcement officers to act with necessary and reasonable force when faced with physical or threatening confrontations. As admirable as the vast majority of officers

FIGURE 9.4: *Officers must analyze situations to eliminate incidents using unreasonable or excessive force.*

are, human error or inappropriate emotional investment may occur and lead to the use of **unreasonable force**. Unreasonable force occurs when the type, degree, and duration of force employed was not necessary or reasonable. Excessive force incidents often create a downward spiral of lawsuits, agency disciplinary action, and disgruntled citizens.

In addition to lawsuits filed against individual officers, an officer's improper use of force can create **vicarious liability**; this means that the agency is legally responsible for the actions performed by its individual officers. The United States Code prohibits police officers from the act of "depriving citizens of their rights under the color of authority" and punishes officials if they disobey regulation.

Necessary Intervention

Intervention from a fellow officer when excessive force is used preserves the integrity and the professionalism of the police force. The case for intervening in the event of such a situation includes the following issues:

- Personal integrity remains intact
- Enhances safety for all involved
- Public confidence is preserved
- Law enforcement's mission is accomplished
- Reduces liability issues

It can be difficult in the heat of the moment to interfere with another police officer's action. In fact, there are multiple reasons why officers do not report or intervene. Often, there are personal friendships between officers, doubts about what is or is not justified, and a sense of "us vs. them" that come into play in these encounters.

Officers are encouraged to trust their own judgment and instinct when a situation is wrong. Consequences of not intervening are commonly more serious than when no intervention was attempted. The increase of stress, threat of a possible lost court case, and risk to a career weighs heavily in a decision to take a stand.

Documenting The Use Of Force

Peace officers are required to report when physical force has been used. Thoroughly and accurately documenting the facts reflects not only upon the officer's own professionalism, but also ensures that the justice system will have all the information it needs to prosecute the case effectively. When documenting a use of force incident, there are two things officers must make note of: the precursory acts that led up to the event and specific fact patterns that were present at the time.

Precursory acts are the details that occur before the encounter, which includes anything from how the officer arrived at the scene to the suspect acknowledging that he or she was in the presence of authority. **Specific fact patterns** are the facts and circumstances that were evident when the type of force was used.

FIGURE 9.5: *Personal friendships should not interfere with an officer's duty to intervene in improper behavior by other law enforcement personnel.*

There are a number of different ways to report a use of force incident, but generally speaking, there are five important points to include.

Factors	A detailed description of what occurred between the officer and the suspect that warranted the use of force. Often includes who, what, where, when, why, and how.
Environment	Keen observation of the physical nature surrounding the confrontation and the probability that the officer may or did have a loss of control
Description	Proper names of force technique; the effect or non-effect from the applied force; the communication before, during, and after
Post-custody	Actions after the suspect had been detained, such as double-locking the handcuffs, any needed medical treatment, and collection of evidence
Statements	Witness recollection from those who viewed the incident or were in close proximity. Interviews should be conducted at the scene with a recording device to ensure accuracy.

FIGURE 9.6: *Methods of reporting a use of force incident.*

Other critical information may include circumstantial details, crime scene details, evidence collection, photographs, witness and subject statements and medical records.

Officers should be prepared to answer questions about their actions. Typically, officers do a good job of documenting their actions; however, defense attorneys often attack an officer's credibility by citing alternative actions the officer could have taken. Officers often aren't prepared to explain why they *didn't* do something. An experienced officer understands the principles of escalation and de-escalation of force, and has a firm knowledge of the use of force policy. Generally, experienced officers are ready to explain why alternative options were not appropriate or reasonable.

Summary

This Module has provided a discussion of a variety of methods that officers may use to assert their authority in order to settle disputes and keep the peace.

A police officer's goal should be to encourage voluntary compliance whenever possible. Sometimes, the actions of a suspect may result in the officer having to respond with force. The officer must take a measured and appropriate response using the skills and tools at hand. The range of response essentially begins with the presence of authority and ends with lethal force. The police have a continuum of force options to guide them in what is appropriate under the conditions they face.

Officers should have knowledge of the reasonable force needed to make an arrest, prevent an escape, and overpower a combative suspect.

Some highlights in this Module include: the obligation to initiate a reasonable means of communication, balancing both professional demeanor and safety requirements; the responsibility for the preservation of human life, as well as dealing with the possibility of having to use deadly force; and the importance of necessary intervention between a colleague and suspect if a situation gets out of control.

Knowing the current laws and agency's policies pertaining to the use of force is paramount to making good decisions. Strong emotions, such as fear and anger, may hinder performance, but with continuous practice, these feelings can be controlled. Staying calm and impartial when in the middle of a dangerous or threatening situation is extremely difficult but manageable.

To reinforce that the police do not take advantage of certain powers, the Supreme Court has made rulings regarding the use of force options.

Sometimes an incident may result in legal action against the officer and agency. A well-documented and accurate report about the use of force encounter offers the best protection for law enforcers.

Discussion Questions

1. What began as a routine jaywalking stop escalated into a loud, confrontational incident that provoked the officer to whack the back of the pedestrian's leg in order to make arrest. Based on what you have read, was this the proper force option used?

2. A suspect pulls a knife on an officer trained in defense techniques, but is outweighed by at least 80 pounds. If the arsenal includes a firearm, baton, pepper spray, and handcuffs, which of these force options should be used first? If you were head of the agency, what set of rules would you establish in such a scenario?

3. An officer responds to a call of "man with a knife" in the park. Upon arrival, the officer approaches a twelve-year-old boy with a hunting knife who is apparently showing it to his friends. As the officer approaches, the boy turns around with the knife in his hand. In this case, would the circumstances merit the officer drawing a firearm? Is the suspect's age a factor? What is the totality of the circumstances?

4. What are some ways that anger can be managed when witnessing a husband beating his wife in front of their child? How important would previous training in managing anger be for an officer who had first-hand experience with domestic violence as a youth? What is the likelihood he or she could administer excessive force?

5. What types of interference would be used when an arresting officer uses the Taser gun a little too long on an unarmed suspect? If the force was deemed unreasonable by the officer's agency, what type of punishment could happen? Who (the individual officer, the witnessing officer or the department) would be legally liable if an accidental death occurred?

Key Terms

Control — With regard to defensive tactics, the ability to maintain or overcome power.

Deadly force — A level of force likely to cause death or serious bodily harm.

Fact specific — All relevant factors that occur during an incident that are documented for police records and possible court hearings.

Force options — Choices available to an officer in each agency's policy to overcome resistance, make an arrest, prevent escape, or to gain control of the situation.

Graham v. Connor — A landmark case in which the U.S. Supreme Court ruled that the law must abide to a specific list to determine reasonable force. Petitioner Graham sustained multiple injuries when officers refused to release him right away, reporting that Graham's behavior was suspicious. In actuality, as a diabetic, Graham refused to wait in a convenience store line and walked away abruptly.

Imminent danger — A threat so significant that a person reasonably believes it will result in death or serious injury.

Intervention — The act of preventing or stopping the inappropriate or unlawful behavior of another.

Justifiable homicide — Under special circumstances, the killing of another human being is considered to be lawful by an officer.

Objective reasonableness — The reason for the use of force must be fact specific and necessary from a reasonable standpoint.

Police brutality — Legal term for a civil rights violation that occurs when a police officer acts with excessive force.

Precursory acts — Events that led up to the encounter with the subject, including how the officer arrived at the scene and what measures were taken when investigations began.

Reasonable fear — Normal response to a potential threat.

Reasonable force — How much and what kind of force an officer may use in a given circumstance.

Reasonable necessity — Delay in custody would create an unreasonable risk to officers, resulting in injury or even death.

Self control — Maintaining composure in order to make sound judgments and decisions.

Serious bodily harm or injury — A serious impairment of physical condition, including, but not limited to, loss of consciousness, concussion, bone fracture, serious disfigurement.

Specific fact patterns — The actual facts of the case, as opposed to prior knowledge, decision-making processes, hypothetical actions, or actions that are not provable.

Tennessee v. Garner — A landmark Supreme Court case. The officers in question fatally shot an unarmed suspected felon, Edward Garner. At the time, it was lawful for an officer to prevent escape by using deadly force. The victim's family argued that the officers violated the victim's Constitutional Rights, and the court ruled that such force was unnecessary. Furthermore, deadly force is only Constitutional if the suspect poses a threat of serious bodily harm either to fellow officers or to others.

Unreasonable fear — Overreaction from unrealistic threats, possibly due to past trauma.

Unreasonable force — A type, degree, and duration of force employed at an unnecessary or inappropriate level.

Vicarious liability — The responsibility of an agency for the conduct of its officers.

MODULE 10

Vehicle Operations

Key Module Concepts:

- Preparing a vehicle for patrol

- Factors contributing to accidents

- Components of vehicle operations

- Estimating stopping distances

- Knowing the effects of speed

- Understanding seatbelt and air bag usage

- Operating a vehicle properly in emergency situations

Introduction

Driving any emergency vehicle requires the operator to be aware of far more issues than those required of the ordinary civilian operator. Avoiding liability is a major priority. Every move by the law enforcement driver is scrutinized by the public and by the officer's superiors. Driving a patrol vehicle demands extreme professionalism and care. Mistakes made behind the wheel of a patrol vehicle can have consequences far beyond those meted out to the civilian driver.

Every time an officer closes the door on a unit and puts the key in the ignition, he puts on one more piece of the uniform. Similar to the pride that most officers take in their uniform and equipment, the vehicle he operates requires, and deserves, the same pride and attention to detail.

As you read, consider these questions:

- *What distinguishes patrol officers' actions from those of civilians when operating a vehicle?*

- *How should driving habits change from those used in a personal vehicle to those used when driving a patrol unit vehicle?*

- *What constitutes a safe driver in law enforcement?*

The Context Of Law Enforcement Driving

Normal Patrol Operation

The bulk of patrol driving will take place during an officer's normal shift. In many ways, normal patrol driving is similar to driving off duty; in other ways, it is significantly different. You will be constantly listening to the radio, trying to stay aware of where other officers in your area are located and what they are doing. The following situations may occur, changing the course of normal patrol operations.

Emergency Response

During an **emergency response**, police dispatchers send officers to locations where people and/or property are in danger. In these situations, officers need to get to the scene as quickly as possible, but without creating a more dangerous situation. You may need to use your emergency lights and siren and disregard certain traffic laws, such as maintaining the speed limit. Emergency response driving will require the use of certain driving techniques to maintain control of your vehicle while operating in emergency mode.

Pursuits

Pursuits — particularly high-speed pursuits — represent one of the most dangerous tasks in law enforcement. Both the officer and the fleeing suspect are at risk, just by virtue of the speeds at which they are driving. In addition, there may be other drivers or pedestrians on the road, as well as other responding officers who must coordinate their actions with the initial officer's. Pursuits (unless terminated early) typically end in one of two ways: in a crash where the suspect loses control of the vehicle, or in a high-risk collision with other vehicles. In either case, the responding officers must be able to quickly switch out of pursuit mode so they can properly and professionally control the outcome.

FIGURE 10.1: *High-speed pursuits can create many hazards and carry many consequences.*

Preparing For Patrol

Driving a law enforcement vehicle, even during normal patrol operations, is not like driving a personal vehicle. Officers never know when they will be called to an emergency response, so vehicles must be checked every day to ensure that the vehicle and its accessories are in proper working order. When driving on patrol, officers are not merely trying to get from Point A to Point B — they are patrolling an area, answering the dispatch radio looking for suspicious activity, keeping an eye out for traffic violators, and scanning for people needing assistance. When weather conditions are so poor that other drivers stay home, law enforcement is still on the road. Remember that the extreme conditions patrol personnel face are not always external — an officer may be fatigued or emotionally stressed from a particularly difficult call. We will look at how to prepare for and conduct basic patrol operation of a vehicle.

Vehicle Inspection

Because a law enforcement vehicle may be used in an emergency response at any moment, it must be in good working order at the beginning of each shift. The pre-operation inspection is especially important if your vehicle is not personally assigned, and another officer has used it since you last drove it. Do not skimp on this inspection — your life, or the lives of others, may depend on your vehicle's ability to function well. Using a vehicle inspection checklist may be helpful. Most departments require officers to use a vehicle inspection checklist, so be sure to follow your department policy when inspecting vehicles.

Check the exterior of the vehicle at the beginning of every shift.

Tires and Wheels

- Are tires inflated to the manufacturer's specifications?
- Is there at least 2/32" tread depth?
- Are there cracks, punctures, or damage to the sidewalls?
- Is the tread unevenly worn?
- Are the rims bent or damaged?
- Are lug nuts tight?
- Are wheel covers in place?

Did You Know?

To check tread depth, insert a penny into the tread. 2/32" is approximately the distance between the top edge of a penny and the top of Lincoln's head.

Body

- Is there new body damage?
- Are any of the windows cracked or otherwise damaged?
- Is any attached equipment, such as windshield wipers or the antenna, damaged?
- Does the suspension appear to be normal (car level)?

Undercarriage

- Are the muffler and tail pipe intact and in good condition?
- Are there any fluid leaks?
- Are there any obvious broken or damaged parts?

Engine

- Check all fluids, including oil, transmission fluid, window-washing fluid, power steering fluid, and brake fluid. Are all fluids at the appropriate levels?"
- Are the battery cables snug?
- Are all hoses and belts in good condition, with no obvious leaks, cracks, or fraying?

Trunk

- Is the spare tire in place and in good condition?
- Are the lug wrench and jack in place?
- Are equipment and supplies in order? (These will vary by agency, but may include such items as a fire extinguisher, first-aid equipment and evidence collection equipment)
- Did the previous user leave any evidence or personal items behind?
- Is everything properly secured?

Passenger Compartment

Before getting in the vehicle, check the passenger compartment to make sure the previous driver or passenger did not leave anything behind. If possible, remove the rear seat, and look under and between the front seats with a flashlight. Do this before every shift and after every transport. If you find a weapon or contraband after transporting a suspect or prisoner, you can be sure it was left by that person.

Make sure the following equipment is working properly:

- Door locks, including buttons that prevent the rear passenger from opening the doors from inside

- Folding/sliding screen/cage between the front and rear seats

- Seatbelts/shoulder harnesses

- Windshield wipers

- Dashboard gauges

- Lights:
    - Headlights, including both high and low beams
    - Emergency lights
    - Alley lights (side-facing) and take-down lights (forward-facing)
    - Spotlights
    - Turn signals
    - Brake lights

- Hazard lights (flashers)
- Interior lights

- Electronics:
  - Radio
  - P.A. system
  - Siren
  - Mobile Data Terminal (MDT)/computer
  - Radar Unit

- Long gun:
  - Does the mount work properly?
  - Is the gun set up as it should be for patrol, with proper ammunition, loaded or unloaded per your agency's policy?

With practice, these checks will take only a few moments. When you consider the consequences of non-functioning equipment, these steps are worth your time and effort. If you do encounter a problem with your vehicle or its equipment, be sure to document it in accordance with your agency's policies.

Accident Factors

While normal patrol driving is similar in some ways to ordinary off-duty driving, in other ways it is very different. This section discusses the aspects of patrol driving that are different than — and more difficult than — civilian driving.

While the conditions listed may not be avoidable, you still can take steps to mitigate the effects. **The single most important choice you can make is to maintain a cushion of space around your vehicle.**

This cushion of space allows adequate time to react to changing conditions. Just as you would maintain distance from a suspect to give yourself time to react appropriately to a sudden assault, you should maintain distance from other vehicles that may endanger your physical well being.

FIGURE 10.2: *"On the job" accidents can result of a number of different factors.*

Multi-Tasking

An officer may be multi-tasking even when she is not using official police equipment. An officer on routine patrol will be scanning the area, looking for signs of unusual activity or other problems. She will also be listening to radio traffic and keeping track of where nearby officers are located. An officer responding to a call will be planning a route, thinking about how to approach the scene, and running various mental scenarios of how to handle the call. Simply put, **multi-tasking** puts you at risk because it divides your attention.

Weather and Road Conditions

When the snow and wind are so bad that officials direct citizens to stay off the roads, law enforcement officers are still on patrol. When it is too foggy to see the road 20 feet ahead, police are still dispatched to calls. When the roads are slick with rain or ice, law enforcement officers still have to drive. Sometimes, the road itself is the problem — it may be undergoing repairs, resulting in broken pavement, lane closures or detours.

When driving conditions are bad, your first response should be to slow down. Unfortunately, one of the by-products of frequent exposure to driving in poor conditions may be overconfidence. The more familiar something becomes, the more it is taken for granted. Driving too fast for current conditions is a common cause of officer accidents. Just as you can never afford to become complacent about officer safety when dealing with suspects, you can never afford to take poor driving conditions for granted.

Night Driving

Law enforcement work is shift work. Much of it is done during the night. While night driving has some advantages, such as less traffic, it is also filled with hazards. It is hard to see at night, even in a well-lit city. On rural roads, it can be even more difficult. Other drivers may blind you with their high beams. It is more difficult to judge the speed of oncoming vehicles at night. As you age, your night vision will get worse, because the pupil will not enlarge as much to let in more light. Here are some guidelines for night driving:

- *Never over-drive your headlights.* Do not drive at a speed that requires a greater stopping distance than the area illuminated by your headlights.

- *Turn off your high beams when following another vehicle.* Do not blind other traffic.

- *Avoid being blinded by other drivers.* If an oncoming driver has forgotten to turn off his high beams, flash your high beams once. If that is not effective, avoid staring into the high beams. Instead, focus on the white stripe on the edge of the pavement (the "fog line") if one is present.

Fatigue

Officers are frequently fatigued from working rotating shifts, putting in overtime after a late dispatch or from making a 9:00 a.m. court appearance after a midnight shift. As a result, fatigue is both part of the job and a major driving hazard. Research shows that sleep deprivation can impair driving as much as intoxication. While you cannot always control fatigue, you can recognize the danger it presents and take some steps to combat it.

If possible, stop frequently to get out of your vehicle and walk around. Vary your routine in some way. Above all, recognize that falling asleep at the wheel can kill you and perhaps others. If you find yourself starting to nod off, *pull over and turn off the vehicle.*

Emotional Factors and Cumulative Stress

Law enforcement is a stressful job. Officers deal with the full range of human activity, from the heart-wrenching to the mundane, often with no time in between calls to recover. An officer may go directly from a grisly homicide to a home where Halloween decorations were stolen, or from a sexual assault to a fender-bender. Sometimes, you have to put your emotions "on hold" while you deal with the situation at hand. While doing so is necessary in the short term, it can be devastating in the long term.

Emotions that are ignored do not go away; they simply manifest in other ways. One sign of cumulative stress is an inability to concentrate, while another common response is irritability. Both can be dangerous. Driving requires concentration, which is already limited by the multi-tasking required for law enforcement work. An irritated driver can quickly become an aggressive driver. Be sure that you find healthy ways to relieve stress and allow your emotions to dissipate. You will feel better, and you will be safer on the job.

Unexpected Hazards

While many unexpected hazardous situations may occur while driving, most of them involve other drivers or conditions out of your control. Two hazards that are within your power to correct are rapid air loss (a "tire blowout") and running off the edge of the roadway.

Rapid Air Loss

If a tire suddenly and rapidly loses air, it can become difficult to control your vehicle. The faster you are traveling, the more difficult it will be to steer. The following procedure outlines the proper way to handle rapid air loss:

- Do *not* apply the brake—it will decrease your ability to steer even more
- Accelerate slightly
- Grip the steering wheel firmly and keep the wheels straight
- Look for a safe place to decelerate
- When your vehicle has slowed, gently apply the brakes and pull off the road

Off-Road Recovery

If your vehicle runs off the edge of the road, the best course of action is simply to slow down and return to the road when it is safe to do so. In some cases, however, you may need to return to the road quickly, follow these steps:

- Position your vehicle so that the wheels are away from the edge of the pavement, and there is room to turn

- Turn the wheels sharply toward the pavement

- As soon as the outside front wheel hits the edge of the pavement, counter-steer to maintain your position in the lane. Even at relatively high speeds, this procedure can usually be accomplished smoothly without loss of control. Do not panic.

Components Of Vehicle Operation

In any driving situation, the driver can actively do only three things to control the vehicle: *steer, accelerate/decelerate,* and *brake.* These three actions are referred to as driver inputs. As you increase any one input, you decrease the effectiveness of the others. This relationship is obvious with acceleration and braking. Many driving situations, however, require you to steer while you accelerate or brake. Remember that you need to balance these inputs for optimum control.

Steering

Normally, the goal in driving is to make your steering as smooth as possible. As you drive, you make constant adjustments in your steering. Much of steering is automatic for an experienced driver. Two aspects, however, should always be conscious choices: changing lanes and passing another vehicle.

When you decide to change lanes, go through the following procedure:

- Make sure you have a cushion of space — preferably at least four seconds — in front of your vehicle in your present lane. Because of the impending lane change, your attention will be momentarily diverted, and the more space you have, the more reaction time you have.

- Assess the relative speed of vehicles in the lane to which you are moving so that you can match speeds

- Check to make sure there is room for your vehicle to fit, with a space cushion, between vehicles in the lane you will be entering. Be sure to check your blind spots before moving.

- Turn on your blinker (turn signal)

- When conditions are right, enter the lane smoothly

If you are passing a slower vehicle on a four-lane highway, the procedure is similar to a two-way lane change: move from the driving lane into the passing lane and back again. Be sure to go through the lane-change procedure for both changes. If you are passing a slower vehicle on a two-lane road, however, you will be crossing into the lane occupied by oncoming traffic. The procedure is slightly different:

- Watch oncoming traffic for an opening that is sufficient for you to pass the slower vehicle. Do not pass on curves, hills, or when approaching intersections. Turn your headlights on to increase visibility.

- When it is safe to do so, turn on your blinker and pull into the oncoming lane. Accelerate smoothly, quickly and safely to the appropriate passing speed.

- Pass the slower vehicle, keeping as far to the left in the oncoming lane as is practical. Do not crowd the slower vehicle.

- When you can see the slower vehicle's headlights in your rear view mirror, signal your intention to move, and return to your original lane

In both situations, your steering should be smooth and controlled, not jerky or abrupt.

Backing

Backing is inherently dangerous, both because your field of view is smaller than when you are driving forward, and because it is more difficult to steer. For ordinary backing, use the following procedure:

- If possible, get out of your vehicle and look behind the car before starting to back it up. Short obstacles such as trashcans that are close to the car may not be visible from the driver's seat.

- Place your left hand at 12 o'clock on the steering wheel. Turn your shoulders and upper body to the right so that you can look over your right shoulder and out the rear window.

- Start to back up slowly and carefully. Use your left hand to steer. To back in a straight line, pick out a spot at a distance that is in line with your intended travel path. Keep looking at your reference point as you back up point as you back. You will find that you will correct the steering automatically. Avoid looking at the pavement directly behind your car; you will find yourself overcorrecting, and you will end up in a zigzag pattern.

- Use your outside mirrors to help you negotiate tight clearances

Cornering

In patrol driving you will encounter all kinds of corners, from residential intersections to curves on major highways. Regardless of the shape of the curve or corner, the same principles apply for safe negotiation. Follow these steps to negotiate a corner safely.

- Evaluate the corner before you arrive there. Check the sharpness of the corner, traffic at intersections, and any other obstacles or obstructions.

- If you are turning at an intersection, activate your turn signal at least 100 feet ahead of the turn

- Position your vehicle for the most efficient turn. If you are on a city street, make right turns from the right lane and left turns from the farthest-left lane.

- If needed, slow down before you enter a curve — braking during a curve or turn diminishes your ability to steer. The entry point, or turn-in, varies with the curve. The sharper the curve or turn, the farther in you have to go before changing direction to steer through the curve. Be careful not to over-steer. In a rear-wheel drive, as little as a 25° turn can cause the rear wheels to overtake the front wheels, leading to a loss of control

- Aim for the apex of the curve, or that point where a straight line drawn from your entry point would just touch the inside edge of your lane

- As you reach the apex, steer smoothly toward your intended exit point and begin to accelerate. To negotiate a curve safely, you must balance **centrifugal force**, which pushes an object outward from the center of rotation and **centripetal force**, which pulls an object into the center of rotation. If either of these dominates the equation, your vehicle will deviate from the desired path. Two things besides steering will affect the balance between centrifugal and centripetal force:

    - **Acceleration:** Acceleration increases centrifugal force. If you accelerate too quickly, you will gravitate toward the outside of the curve.

    - **Weight transfer:** When a vehicle changes direction or speed, weight transfer occurs. As you accelerate, the front end of your vehicle lifts, transferring weight to the rear. In a rear-wheel drive vehicle, this will increase traction, but in a front-wheel drive vehicle, it will decrease traction.

Similarly, as you brake, the front end drops, transferring weight to the front wheels, increasing their already high braking efficiency — and potentially causing the brakes to "lock up." As you change direction, the weight transfers from side to side. If the speed is too high, and the turn too sharp, the vehicle could roll over.

When the car is at rest, the car's weight is evenly distributed, and it is most stable. This is also true of a car moving at a constant speed in a straight line.

Braking

The average American driver relies too heavily on braking as a response to emergencies, rather than using evasive maneuvers or other techniques. In addition, most people greatly underestimate required stopping distances. As a result, braking is frequently uncontrolled, resulting in panic braking that is inefficient and dangerous. This section discusses the techniques for different sorts of braking, as well as the factors affecting stopping distance. Certain principles apply to safe braking:

- **Avoid following closely behind other vehicles**. The bigger your cushion of space, the more time you have to react to a situation and the more distance you have in which to stop

- **Avoid left-foot braking**. Using your left foot on the brake encourages "riding" the brakes. This can cause brake "fade" or failure, premature wear, and confusion for the driver behind you, who sees your brake lights on all the time.

- **Be aware of traffic behind you when you begin braking**. The tighter the traffic, the more slowly you must brake to avoid being rear-ended. Check traffic to the sides to see if you have an escape path if needed. In normal patrol driving, you will use various braking techniques, depending on the situation. Normal braking falls into two general categories: controlled braking and sudden stops.

Controlled Braking

Controlled braking takes place whenever you have control of the stopping distance. Controlled braking allows you to slow the vehicle smoothly, without being concerned that you will lock the wheels. If you break hard enough to lock the wheels, you lose significant traction. In controlled braking, you will use two basic techniques:

- **Early and smooth braking**: Apply steady, constant pressure early and then smoothly release pressure and the vehicle slows to a stop

- **Trail braking**: Gradually reduce brake pressure after you have begun to turn into a corner

Sudden Stops

There are times when you cannot control braking distance. For example, when a pedestrian darts into traffic in front of you, or the car directly in front of you is involved in an accident, you need to be able to bring your vehicle to a stop in the shortest possible time. There are three techniques for this.

- **ABS brakes**: If your vehicle is equipped with anti-lock brakes, apply steady, firm pressure until the vehicle stops. Most anti-lock braking systems have computerized sensors that detect when the wheel is about to lock-up and release the brake momentarily. The brakes may pulsate up to 15 times a second. (Certain road conditions, such as the presence of soft, accumulated material like snow or gravel, or irregular surfaces like railroad tracks, steel grates, or rough, "washboard" surfaces will "fool" the computer into thinking the wheels have locked and may result in a longer stopping distance.) Note that if the ABS system fails, the vehicle will normally revert to standard braking.

- **"Threshold braking"**: Apply maximum brake pressure until just before lock-up, and then maintain that pressure. This provides the maximum braking power, but maintains steering and traction.

- **"Lock-up"**: In this case, you apply maximum brake pressure until lock-up occurs, and then release the pressure and try to maintain threshold braking. The disadvantage of this technique is that, because of the problems with steering and traction, it is difficult to predict how long the wheels will remain locked up. Any time the wheels lock up, you have decreased control of the vehicle, although the specific effects differ.

  - **Front wheels locked**: This is caused by improper brake adjustment or slick spots on the road. Braking ability is reduced, traction is reduced, and the car begins to slide. The rear wheels, which are still turning, act as a rudder, keeping the car moving straight ahead.

  - **Rear wheels locked**: This condition is caused by improper brake adjustment. The rear wheels, which are sliding, will start to overtake the front wheels and try to lead the car. The vehicle may start to rotate. The driver must counter-steer and reduce brake pressure to control the vehicle.

  - **All wheels locked**: This situation is caused by panic braking, in which the driver applies too much pressure to the brakes. As long as the road surface, tire pressure, and tire tread are fairly even, the car will most likely skid forward in a straight line.

Stopping Distance

The distance required to bring a vehicle to a complete stop varies due to a number of factors. In physical terms, stopping distance is determined by the combination of kinetic energy, driver reaction time, vehicle capability, and environmental conditions.

Kinetic energy is a function of mass and velocity. The heavier the vehicle, and the faster it is going, the more distance will be required to stop. Note that kinetic energy increases as the square of the velocity — in other words, a vehicle going twice as fast as another will take four times the distance to stop, all other factors being equal. Other factors of stopping distance are listed in Figure 10.3.

Determining Factor	Cause
Driver reaction time	Perception/anticipation of the need to stop Attitude and emotional control Concentration Skill Physiological reaction limits Physiological impairment
Vehicle capability	Brake system Suspension system Tires
Environmental conditions	Road surface Road design Weather conditions Direction of road (uphill vs. downhill)

FIGURE 10.3: *Various factors and causes relating to stopping distance.*

Most people greatly underestimate the distance required to bring their vehicle to a controlled stop. Practice leaving a large cushion of space in front of you to give yourself the stopping distance you need.

Seatbelt Use

There are no valid excuses for not wearing a seatbelt. Once you buckle in, be sure that you are wearing it properly. Make sure that your lap belt is placed across the strongest portion of your hips. Your shoulder strap should fit between your neck and end of your shoulder. Once you've positioned the seatbelt correctly, make sure that it is snug across your body by grabbing your shoulder strap and pulling it up toward the roof. A loose belt could allow a person to slide underneath it. By the time the lap belt finally begins to work, it has already moved up onto the stomach, where there are only flesh and internal organs to stop it. This can cause internal damage and lead to death.

What Happens When Air Bags Deploy?

Air bags are typically designed to deploy in frontal and near-frontal collisions, which are comparable to hitting a solid barrier at approximately 8 to 14 miles per hour (mph). Roughly speaking, a 14 mph barrier collision is equivalent to striking a parked car of similar size across the full front of each vehicle at about 28 mph. This is because the parked car absorbs some of the energy of the crash as it is pushed by the striking vehicle. Unlike crash tests into barriers, real-world crashes typically occur at angles, and the crash forces usually are not evenly distributed across the front of the vehicle. Consequently, the relative speed between a striking and struck vehicle required to deploy the air bag in a real-world crash can be much higher than an equivalent barrier crash.

Because air bag sensors measure deceleration, vehicle speed and damage are not good indicators of whether or not an air bag should deploy. Occasionally, air bags can deploy due to the vehicle's undercarriage violently striking an object protruding above the road's surface. Despite the lack of visible front-end damage, high deceleration forces may occur in this type of crash, resulting in the deployment of the air bag.

Most air bags are designed to deploy automatically in the event of a vehicle fire when temperatures reach 300 to 400 degrees Fahrenheit. This safety feature helps to ensure that such temperatures do not cause an explosion of the inflator unit within the air bag module.

Front air bags are not designed to deploy in side impact, rear impact, or rollover crashes. Since air bags deploy only once and deflate quickly after the initial impact, they will not be beneficial during a subsequent collision. Seat belts help reduce the risk of injury in many types of crashes. They help to position occupants properly to maximize the air bags' benefits, and they help restrain occupants during the initial and subsequent collisions. It is extremely important that safety belts are always worn, even in air-bag equipped vehicles.

FIGURE 10.4: *Air bags have become an essential part of vehicle safety.*

Three Separate Collisions In One

In both minor and serious crashes, there are three separate collisions. They are the vehicle collision, the human collision, and the internal collision.

The Vehicle Collision

During a collision, a vehicle will come to a violent and sudden stop while making contact with an object. If you are traveling at 50 mph and hit a tree, your vehicle will come to a complete stop in a split second. At 30 mph, a vehicle hitting a stationary object will crumple inward about two feet. As the vehicle crushes, it absorbs some of the force of the collision.

The Human Collision

At the moment of impact, the occupants are still traveling at the vehicle's speed. When the vehicle stops, the occupants continue to be hurled forward until they make contact with some part of the car. They will strike the steering wheel, dashboard, front window, or back of the front seat. Occupants can also collide with each other with great force, causing serious injury.

The Internal Collision

The internal organs of the human body continue to move in the aftermath of a crash, causing an internal collision that can result in serious injury or death. **Coup injury** is the result of a sudden, violent stop that causes the brain to accelerate forward and hit the front or side of the skull. It is usually the result of an object striking the head, and will present a contusion at the site of impact. A **contra coup injury** occurs when the brain accelerates forward, hits the inside of the skull, and then bounces off the other side of the skull. A contra coup injury is often the result of the head striking an object, and will present a contusion on the opposite side of impact. In both cases, the brain is damaged as it rubs against the inner ridges of the skull. A brain that undergoes a particularly violent and sudden impact can experience both a coup and a contra coup injury.

Common causes of coup and contra coup injury include:

- Car accidents
- Assault
- Shaken baby syndrome
- Falls
- Sports and athletic injuries

Vehicle Operations In Emergency Situations

As stated earlier, officers must drive with due regard when using emergency equipment and while looking for potential hazards on the roads. Some points to remember include the following:

- Use your siren well in advance. Change the siren pitch to attract the attention of the inattentive motorist.

- Slow down and approach intersections with caution, especially when you have a congested or obstructed view of the intersection

- Anticipate potential problems, such as pedestrians crossing the road, or drivers in parked vehicles who may open their door to exit the vehicle or pull out into the roadway

- When operating at higher speeds on rural roadways, watch for livestock, farm machinery, or other slow-moving vehicles moving along the side the roadway

- On freeways and interstate highways, execute and plan lane changes well in advance and drive in the left-hand lane

- Remember your siren is ineffective at freeway speeds, so motorists may not hear you coming up behind them

Summary

Law enforcement vehicle operation is different than everyday civilian vehicle operation, and requires more training, planning and care. Careful and safe vehicle operations begin before the shift even starts. Adequate rest, the right equipment, the correct vehicle checkout, and the appropriate driving techniques are all important factors in proper vehicle operations. The responsibility for the vehicle does not end with your shift. The vehicle should be fueled, cleaned and readied for the next operator. Make sure to report any maintenance issues as well.

Emergency response represents a very hazardous area for law enforcement — both from the actual dangers and from the liability exposure. Therefore, it presents many challenges. Because of increased stress from the nature of the call and the increased speed of response, emergency response requires great concentration and alertness.

Remember that your responsibility to show due regard for the safety of others overrides all other concerns — get to the emergency quickly, but not at the expense of getting there safely.

Discussion Questions

1. What constitutes good patrol vehicle preparation?

2. What are the three types of driving that officers do in the line of duty?

3. Name two unexpected hazards you might encounter while driving a patrol vehicle.

4. What are the four components of vehicle operation?

5. What are ABS brakes, and how do they work?

6. In a crash, what is the mechanical cause of brain injury?

7. During an emergency response on a freeway, what lane should an officer use?

8. What are the five factors that can contribute to accidents?

Key Terms

Anti-lock brakes (ABS) — Computer operated brakes which are designed to keep wheels from "locking up" and prevent skidding.

Centripetal force — A force that pulls an object into the center of rotation.

Centrifugal force — A force that pushes an object outward from the center of rotation.

Contra coup injury — Occurs when the brain accelerates forward, hits the inside of the skull, and then bounces off the other side of the skull.

Coup injury — The result of a sudden, violent stop that causes the brain to accelerate forward and hit the inside front of the skull.

Due regard — The standard by which every law enforcement officer is measured in terms of his safe or unsafe conduct. In a situation where due regard is shown, a reasonably careful person, performing similar duties under similar circumstances, would act in the same manner.

Emergency response — A response to a call at higher than normal speeds while operating sirens and emergency lights.

Multi-tasking — Performing multiple tasks simultaneously.

Pursuits — A high-speed vehicle chase by law enforcement.

Trail braking — Involves gradually reducing brake pressure after you have begun to turn into a corner.

Weight transfer — A force that transfers weight to the rear of the vehicle on acceleration or to the front when braking.

CPSIA information can be obtained
at www.ICGtesting.com
Printed in the USA
BVHW090914221218

536138BV00015B/54/P